Unit II

Writing Projects

Phil Schlemmer

Illustrated by Patricia A. Sussman

LEARNING ON YOUR OWN!

Individual, Group, and Classroom
Research Projects for
Gifted and Motivated Students

The Center for Applied Research in Education, Inc.
West Nyack, New York

© 1987 by

THE CENTER FOR APPLIED
RESEARCH IN EDUCATION, INC.

West Nyack, N.Y.

Library of Congress Cataloging-in-Publication Data

Schlemmer, Phillip L.
  Writing projects.

  (Learning on your own! ; unit 2)
  1. Gifted children—Education—Language arts
(Elementary) 2. Gifted children—Education—Creative
writing. 3. Project method in teaching. 4. Independent
study. 5. Teacher participation in curriculum planning.
I. Title. II. Series: Schlemmer, Philip L. Learning
on your own!
LC3993.27S34 1987   371.95'3   86-17586

ISBN 0-87628-511-6

PRINTED IN THE UNITED STATES OF AMERICA

Dedication

This book is dedicated to my wife, Dori. Without her unending support, tireless editorial efforts, thoughtful criticisms, and patience, I could not have finished my work. Thank you, Dori.

Acknowledgments

My collaborator and co-teacher for eight years, Dennis Kretschman, deserves special mention at this juncture. Together we developed the activities, projects, and courses that became a "learning to learn" curriculum. Dennis designed and taught several of the projects described in these pages, and he added constantly to the spirit and excitement of an independent learning philosophy that gradually evolved into this set of five books. I deeply appreciate the contribution Dennis has made to my work.

I would also like to thank the following people for their advice, support, and advocacy: J. Q. Adams; Dr. Robert Barr; Robert Cole, Jr.; Mary Dalheim; Dr. John Feldhusen; David Humphrey; Bruce Ottenweller; Dr. William Parrett; Ed Saunders; Charles Whaley; and a special thanks to all the kids who have attended John Ball Zoo School since I started working on this project: 1973–1985.

About the Author

PHIL SCHLEMMER, M.Ed., has been creating and teaching independent learning projects since 1973, when he began his master's program in alternative education at Indiana University. Assigned to Grand Rapids, Michigan, for his internship, he helped develop a full-time school for 52 motivated sixth graders. The school was located at the city zoo and immediately became known as the "Zoo School." This program became an experimental site where he remained through the 1984–85 school year, with one year out as director of a high school independent study program.

Presently working as a private consultant, Mr. Schlemmer has been presenting in-services and workshops to teachers, parents, administrators, and students for more than 13 years and has published articles in *Phi Delta Kappan* and *Instructor.*

Foreword

This series of books will become invaluable aids in programs for motivated, gifted, and talented children. They provide clear guidelines and procedures for involving these children in significant learning experiences in research and high level thinking skills while not neglecting challenging learning within the respective basic disciplines of science, mathematics, social studies, and writing. The approach is one that engages the interests of children at a deep level. I have seen Phil Schlemmer at work teaching with the materials and methods presented in these books and have been highly impressed with the quality of learning which was taking place. While I recognized Phil is an excellent teacher, it nevertheless seemed clear that the method and the materials were making a strong and significant contribution to the children's learning.

Children will learn how to carry out research and will become independent lifelong learners through the skills acquired from the program of studies presented in these books. Success in independent study and research and effective use of libraries and other information resources are not simply products of trial-and-error activity in school. They are products of teacher guidance and stimulation along with instructional materials and methods and an overall system which provides the requisite skills and attitudes.

All of the material presented in this series of books has undergone extensive tryout. The author has also spent thousands of hours developing, writing, revising, and editing, but above all he has spent his time conceptualizing and designing a dynamic system for educating motivated, gifted, and talented youth. The net result is a program of studies which should make an invaluable contribution to the education of these youth. And, above all that, I am sure that if it is taught well, the kids will love it.

John F. Feldhusen, Ph.D., Director
Gifted Education Resource Institute
Purdue University
West Lafayette, Indiana 47907

About Learning on Your Own!

In the summer of 1973, I was offered the opportunity of a lifetime. The school board in Grand Rapids, Michigan authorized a full-time experimental program for 52 motivated sixth-grade children, and I was asked to help start it. The school was described as an environmental studies program, and its home was established in two doublewide house trailers that were connected and converted into classrooms. This building was placed in the parking lot of Grand Rapids' municipal zoo (John Ball Zoological Gardens). Naturally, the school came to be known as "The Zoo School."

The mandate for the Zoo School staff was clear—to build a challenging, stimulating, and interesting curriculum that was in no way limited by the school system's stated sixth-grade objectives. Operating with virtually no textbooks or "regular" instructional materials, we had the freedom to develop our own projects and courses, schedule our own activities, and design our own curriculum.

Over a period of ten years, hundreds of activities were created to use with motivated learners. This was a golden opportunity because few teachers are given a chance to experiment with curriculum in an isolated setting with the blessing of the school board. When a project worked, I wrote about it, recorded the procedures that were successful, filed the handouts, and organized the materials so that someone else could teach it. The accumulation of projects for motivated children led to a book proposal which, in turn, led to this five-book series. *Learning on Your Own!* is based entirely on actual classroom experience. Every project and activity has been used successfully with children in the areas of

- Research Skills
- Writing
- Science
- Mathematics
- Social Studies

As the books evolved and materialized over the years, it seemed that they would be useful to classroom teachers, especially in the upper and elementary and junior high grades. This became increasingly clear as teachers from a wide variety of settings were presented with ideas from the books. Teachers saw different uses for the projects, based upon the abilities of their students and their own curricular needs.

Learning on Your Own! will be useful to you for any of the following reasons:

- If a curricular goal is to teach children to be independent learners, then skill development is necessary. The projects in each book are arranged according to the level of independence that is required—the early projects can be used to *teach* skills; the later ones require their *use*.
- These projects prepare the way for students confidently to make use of higher-level thinking skills.
- A broad range of students can benefit from projects that are skill-oriented. They need not be gifted/talented.
- On the other hand, teachers of the gifted/talented will see that the emphasis on independence and higher-level thinking makes the projects fit smoothly into their curricular goals.
- The projects are designed for use by one teacher with a class of up to 30 students. They are intentionally built to accommodate the "regular" class-room teacher. Projects that require 1-to-1 or even 1-to-15 teacher-student ratios are of little use to most teachers.
- The books do not represent a curriculum that must be followed. Gifted/talented programs may have curricula based upon the five-book series, and individual situations may allow for the development of a "learning to learn" curriculum. Generally speaking, however, each project is self-contained and need not be a part of a year-long progression of courses and projects.
- Each project offers a format that can be used even if the *content* is changed. You may, with some modification, apply many projects toward subject material that is already being taught. This provides a means of delivering the same message in a different way.
- Most teachers have students in their classes capable of pursuing projects that are beyond the scope of the class as a whole. These books can be used to provide special projects for such students so that they may learn on their own.
- One of the most pervasive concepts in *Learning on Your Own!* is termed "kids teaching kids." Because of the emphasis placed on students teaching one another, oral presentations are required for many projects. This reinforces the important idea that not only can students *learn,* they can also *teach.* Emphasis on oral presentation can be reduced if time constraints demand it.
- The premise of this series is that children, particularly those who are motivated to learn, need a base from which to expand their educational horizons. Specifically, this base consists of five important components of independent learning:

—skills

—confidence

—a mandate to pursue independence

—projects that show students *how* to learn on their own

—an opportunity to practice independent learning

Learning on Your Own! places primary emphasis on the motivated learner, the definition of which is left intentionally ambiguous. It is meant to include most normal children who have natural curiosities and who understand the need for a good education. Motivated children are important people who deserve recognition for their ability and desire to achieve. The trend toward understanding the special needs and incredible potential of children who enjoy the adventure and challenge of learning is encouraging. Teachers, parents, business people, community leaders, and concerned citizens are beginning to seriously ask, "What can we do for these young people who want to learn?"

Creating a special program or developing a new curriculum is not necessarily the answer. Many of the needs of these children can be met in the regular classroom by teaching basic independent learning skills. No teacher can possibly master and teach all of the areas that his or her students may be interested in studying, but every teacher has opportunities to place emphasis on basic learning skills. A surprising number of children become more motivated as they gain skills that allow them to learn independently. "Learning on your own" is an important concept because it, in itself, provides motivation. You can contribute to your students' motivation by emphasizing self-confidence and skill development. One simple project during a semester can give students insight into the usefulness of independent learning. One lesson that emphasizes a skill can bring students a step closer to choosing topics, finding information, planning projects, and making final presentations without assistance. By teaching motivated students *how to learn on their own,* you give them the ability to challenge themselves, to transcend the six-hour school day.

Beyond meeting the immediate needs of individual students, teaching children how to learn on their own will have an impact on their adult lives and may affect society itself. It is easy to discuss the day-to-day importance of independent learning in one breath, and in the next be talking of the needs of adults 30 years from now. This five-book series is based upon the assumption that educating children to be independent learners makes sense in a complicated, rapidly changing, unpredictable world. Preparing today's children for tomorrow's challenges is of paramount importance to educators and parents, but a monumental task lies in deciding what can be taught that will have lasting value in years to come. What will people need to know in the year 2001 and beyond? Can we accurately prescribe a set of facts and information that will be *necessary* to an average citizen 10, 20, or 30 years from now? Can we feel confident that what we teach will be useful, or even relevant, by the time our students become adults? Teaching children to be independent learners is a compelling response to these difficult, thought-provoking questions.

How to Use
Learning on Your Own!

Learning on Your Own! can be used in many ways. The projects and the overall design of the books lend themselves to a variety of applications, such as basic skill activities, full-class units or courses, small-group projects, independent study, and even curriculum development. Regardless of how the series is to be implemented, it is important to understand its organization and recognize what it provides. Like a good cookbook, this series supplies more than a list of ingredients. It offers suggestions, advice, and hints; provides organization and structure; and gives time lines, handouts, and materials lists. In other words, it supplies everything necessary for you to conduct the projects.

These books were produced with you in mind. Every project is divided into three general sections to provide uniformity throughout the series and to give each component a standard placement in the material. The first section, Teacher Preview, gives a brief overview of the scope and focus of the project. The second section, Lesson Plans and Notes, outlines a detailed, hour-by-hour description. After reading this, every nuance of the project should be understood. The third section, Instructional Materials, supplies the "nuts-and-bolts" of the project— reproducible assignment sheets, instructional handouts, tests, answer sheets, and evaluations.

Here is a concise explanation of each of the three sections. Read this material before going further to better understand how the projects can be used.

Teacher Preview

The Teacher Preview is a quick explanation of what a project accomplishes or teaches. It is divided into seven areas, each of which provides specific information about the project:

Length of Project: The length of each project is given in classroom hours. It does not take into account homework or teacher-preparation time.

Level of Independence: Each project is identified as "basic," "intermediate," or "advanced" in terms of how much independence is required of students. The level of independence is based primarily on how many decisions a student must make and how much responsibility is required. It is suggested that students who have not acquired independent learning skills, regardless of their grade level, be carefully introduced to advanced projects.

For teachers who are interested, there is a correlation between the skill development mentioned here and the progression to higher-level thinking skills typified by Benjamin Bloom's "Taxonomy of Educational Objectives":

Level of Independence	*Bloom's Taxonomy*
Basic	Knowledge
	Comprehension
Intermediate	Application
	Analysis
Advanced	Synthesis
	Evaluation

Goals: These are straightforward statements of what a project is designed to accomplish. Goals that recur throughout the series deal with skill development, independent learning, and "kids teaching kids."

During This Project Students Will: This is a list of concise project objectives. Occasionally, some of these statements become activities rather than objectives, but they are included because they help specify what students will do during the course of a project.

Skills: Each project emphasizes a specific set of skills, which are listed in this section. Further information about the skills is provided in the "Skills Chart." You may change the skill emphasis of a project according to curricular demands or the needs of the students.

Handouts Provided: The handouts provided with a project are listed by name. This includes assignment sheets, informational handouts, tests, and evaluation forms.

Project Calendar: This is a chart that graphically shows each hour of instruction. Since it does not necessarily represent consecutive days, lines are provided for you to pencil in dates. The calendar offers a synopsis of each hour's activity and also brief notes to clue you about things that must be done:

PREPARATION REQUIRED	STUDENTS TURN IN WORK
NEED SPECIAL MATERIALS	RETURN STUDENT WORK
HANDOUT PROVIDED	ANSWER SHEET PROVIDED

Lesson Plans and Notes

The lesson plan is a detailed hour-by-hour description of a project, explaining its organization and presentation methods. Projects can be shortened by reducing the time spent on such things as topic selection, research, and presentation; however, this necessitates de-emphasizing skills that make real independent study possible. Alternately, a project may require additional hours if students are weak in particular skill areas or if certain concepts are not thoroughly understood.

Each hour's lesson plan is accompanied by notes about the project. Some notes are fairly extensive if they are needed to clarify subject matter or describe a process.

Instructional Material

There are five types of reproducible instructional materials included in *Learning on Your Own!* Most projects can be run successfully with just a Student Assignment Sheet; the rest of the materials are to be used as aids at your discretion.

Student Assignment Sheets: Virtually every project has an assignment sheet that explains the project and outlines requirements.

Additional Handouts: Some projects offer other handouts to supply basic information or provide a place to record answers or research data.

Tests and Quizzes: Tests and quizzes are included with projects that present specific content. Since most projects are individualized, the activities themselves are designed to test student comprehension and skill development.

Evaluation Sheets: Many projects provide their own evaluation sheets. In addition, the Teacher's Introduction to the Student Research Guide (see the Appendix) contains evaluations for writing notecards, posters, and oral presentations. Some projects also supply self-evaluation forms so that students can evaluate their own work.

Forms, Charts, Lists: These aids are provided throughout the series. They are designed for specific situations in individual projects.

OTHER FEATURES OF
LEARNING ON YOUR OWN!

In addition to the projects, each book in the series offers several other useful features:

Grade Level: A grade level notation of upper elementary, junior high, and/or high is shown next to each project in the table of contents. Because this series was developed with gifted/talented/motivated sixth graders, junior high is the logical grade level for most projects; thus, generally speaking, these projects are most appropriate for students in grades 6–8.

Skills Chart: This is a chart listing specific independent learning skills that may be applied to each project. It is fully explained in its introductory material.

Teacher's Introduction to the Student Research Guide: This introduction is found in the Appendix. It offers suggestions for conducting research projects and provides several evaluation forms.

Student Research Guide: Also found in the Appendix, this is a series of checklists that can be used by students working on individualized projects. The Daily Log, for example, is a means of having students keep track of their own progress. In addition to the checklists, there are instructional handouts on basic research skills.

General Notes

Examine the *structure* of the projects in each book, even if the titles do not fit specific needs. Many projects are so skill-oriented that content can be drastically altered without affecting the goals.

Many projects are dependent upon resource materials; the more sources of information, the better. Some ways of providing materials for the classroom are to

- Ask parents for donations of books and magazines.
- Advertise for specific materials in the classified section of the newspaper.
- Check out library materials for a mini-library in the classroom.
- Gradually purchase useful materials as they are discovered.
- Take trips to public libraries and make use of school libraries.

Students may not initially recognize the value of using notecards. They will soon learn, however, that the cards allow data to be recorded as individual facts that can be arranged and rearranged at will.

"Listening" is included as an important skill in most projects. In lecture situations, class discussions, and when students are giving presentations, you should require students to listen and respect the right of others to listen.

Provide time for grading and returning materials to students during the course of a project. The Project Calendar is convenient for planning a schedule.

A visual display is often a requirement for projects in this series. Students usually choose to make a poster, but there are other possibilities:

mural	collage	demonstration	dramatization
mobile	model	display or exhibit	book, magazine, or pamphlet
diorama	puppet show	slide show	

When students work on their own, your role changes from information supplier to learning facilitator. It is also important to help students solve their own problems so that momentum and forward progress are maintained.

A FINAL NOTE FROM THE AUTHOR

Learning on Your Own! provides the materials and the structure that are necessary for individualized learning. The only missing elements are the enthusiasm, vitality, and creative energy that are needed to ignite a group of students and set them diligently to work on projects that require concentration and perseverance. I hope that *my* work will make *your* work easier by letting you put your efforts into quality and innovation. The ability to learn independently is perhaps the greatest gift that can be conferred upon students. Give it with the knowledge that it is valuable beyond price, uniquely suited to each individual, and good for a lifetime!

Phil Schlemmer

About This Book

One of the three R's, writing is in danger of becoming an extinct basic skill in these days of video and audio communication. Although students who have instant access to the world through television and computers are often skeptical about the need for writing skills, writing *is* important.

The ultimate goal of these writing projects is to encourage self-expression. Although students are steeped in the wonders of the communications revolution, they are primarily passive receivers—television, video, stereo, radio, computer, and intercontinental satellite communication *give* information to students, but what option is available if *they* want to give information to *others*? One answer, of course, is writing. Writing is not passive; it is an active effort to transmit information and opinions.

The first five projects in this book (Imaginary Words, The Parts of Speech, Writing Reports, Writing Essays, and Writing Letters) emphasize such basic writing skills as grammar, sentences, paragraphs, and parts of speech. Until students recognize the need for good writing skills, the quality of their independently written reports, stories, and essays may be below what they are capable of. It is equally important to emphasize basic skills with motivated children as it is with nonmotivated children—with the acquisition of skills, these students can proceed to the enjoyable task of creative, individualized writing.

The final eight projects (Creative Writing, Story Writing, Roots, Classroom Productions, Book Reports, Class Newspaper, Research/Report Projects, and Year in Review) place primary emphasis on students independently gathering information and putting facts, opinions, and commentaries into written form. These projects are designed to be challenging and interesting; they should help provide the motivation that is often lacking when students are implored to produce their best-written work.

Notice that the four projects (The Fifty States of America, Foreign Countries, The World of Science, and Inventions and Discoveries) listed under Research/Report Projects are all very similar in structure; you will probably want to offer only one of these projects to a group of students in any given semester as more than one may seem redundant. Moreover, if the subject material does not fit your needs, change the topics to create new projects. It is important to recognize that this book offers several project models; the projects can be changed by substituting your own subject material into the models that are provided.

Writing is the key to individualized communication. The process of teaching students to be writers is not easy, even for an experienced teacher who understands that a product is always preceded by a process. In this case, the ability to write must be preceded by the acquisition of skills and the motivation to communicate in writing, which is what this book is all about.

THE SKILLS CHART

Writing Projects is based upon skill development. The projects are arranged according to the amount of independence required, and a list of skills is provided for every project in the book. A comprehensive Skills Chart is included here to help define the skill requirements of each project. Many of them are basic, common-sense skills that are already being taught in your classes.

The Skills Chart is divided into seven general skill areas: research, writing, planning, problem solving, self-discipline, self-evaluation, and presentation. Reading is not included on the chart because it is assumed that reading skills will be used with virtually every project.

The key tells if a skill is prerequisite (#), primary (X), secondary (0), or optional (*) for each project in the book. These designations are based upon the way the projects were originally taught; you may want to shift the skill emphasis of a project to fit the needs of your particular group of students. It is entirely up to you to decide how to present a project and what skills to emphasize. The Skills Chart is only a guide.

Examination of the chart quickly shows which skills are important to a project and which ones may be of secondary value. A project may be changed or rearranged to redirect its skill requirements. The projects in this book are designed to *teach* the use of skills. If a project's Teacher Preview lists twenty skills, but you want to emphasize only three or four of them, that is a perfectly legitimate use of the project.

Evaluating students on their mastery of skills often involves subjective judgments; each student should be evaluated according to his or her *improvement* rather than by comparison with others. Several projects supply evaluation forms to help with this process. In addition, the Teacher's Introduction to the Student Research Guide provides evaluations for notecards, posters, and oral presentations.

A blank Skills Chart is included at the end of the Student Research Guide in the Appendix. This chart can be helpful in several ways:

• Students can chart their own skill progression through a year. Give them a chart and tell them to record the title of a project on the first line. Have them mark the skills *you* have decided to emphasize with the project. This way, students will see *exactly* what skills are being taught and which ones they are expected to know how to use. As projects are continued through the year, the charts will indicate skill development.

• Use the chart to organize the skill emphasis of projects that did not come from this book. Quite often, projects have the potential to teach skills, but they are not organized to do so. An entire course or even a curriculum can be organized according to the skill development on the chart.

• The Skills Chart can be used as a method of reporting to parents. By recording the projects and activities undertaken during a marking period in the left-hand column, a mark for each of the 48 skills can be given. For example, a number system can be used:

1—excellent

2—very good

3—good

4—fair

5—poor

• A simpler method of reporting to parents is to give them a copy of the Skills Chart without marks and use it as the basis for a discussion about skill development.

Finally, most teachers have little or no experience teaching some of the skills listed on the chart. There is plenty of room for experimentation in the field of independent learning, and there are no established "correct" methods of teaching such concepts as problem solving, self-evaluation, and self-discipline. These are things that *can* be taught, but your own teaching style and philosophy will dictate how you choose to do it. The skills listed on this chart should be recognizable as skills that are worth teaching, even if you have not previously emphasized them.

SKILLS CHART: WRITING

Legend:

*Prerequisite Skills* — Students must have command of these skills.

X *Primary Skills* — Students will learn to use these skills; they are necessary to the project.

0 *Secondary Skills* — These skills may play an important role in certain cases.

* *Optional Skills* — These skills may be emphasized but are not required.

	RESEARCH									WRITING						PLANNING				
	BIBLIOGRAPHIES	COLLECTING DATA	INTERVIEWING	WRITING LETTERS	LIBRARY SKILLS	LISTENING	MAKING NOTECARDS	OBSERVING	SUMMARIZING	GRAMMAR	HANDWRITING	NEATNESS	PARAGRAPHS	SENTENCES	SPELLING	GROUP PLANNING	ORGANIZING	OUTLINING	SETTING OBJECTIVES	TOPIC SELECTION
THE PARTS OF SPEECH										X	X	X	*	X	X					
IMAGINARY WORDS										X	X	X	*	X	X					
WRITING REPORTS	X	X	*	*	0		0		X	X	X	X	X	X	X	*	X	X		X
WRITING ESSAYS	*	X	X	*	*	X	*		X	X	X	X	X	X	X	*	X	X		X
WRITING LETTERS		*		X		0				X	X	X	X	X	X	*	X	X		0
CREATIVE WRITING						0				X	X	X	X	X	X		X	X		X
STORY WRITING					X			X		X	X	X	X	X	X		X	X		X
ROOTS		X	X	*	*	X			X	X	X	X	X	X	X		X	X	0	X
CLASSROOM PRODUCTIONS	X	X	X	*	X	X	X	0	X	X	X	X	X	X	X	X	X	0	X	X
BOOK REPORTS	*	0			0				X	X	X	X	X	X	X		X	0	0	X
CLASS NEWSPAPER	X	X	X	*	X	0	*		X	X	X	X	X	X	X	X	X	0	0	X
THE FIFTY STATES OF U.S.A.	#	X	*	X	#	0	#	0	X	X	X	X	#	#	X	*	X	#	X	X
FOREIGN COUNTRIES	#	X	*	X	#	0	#	0	X	X	X	X	#	#	X	*	X	#	X	X
THE WORLD OF SCIENCE	#	X	*	X	#	0	#	0	X	X	X	X	#	#	X	*	X	#	X	X
INVENTIONS & DISCOVERIES	#	X	*	X	#	0	#	0	X	X	X	X	#	#	X	*	X	#	X	X
YEAR IN REVIEW	*	#	X	*	*	X	*	0	X	#	X	X	#	#	X	X	X	#	X	#

SKILLS CHART: WRITING

PROBLEM SOLVING					SELF-DISCIPLINE										SELF-EVALUATION				PRESENTATION								
DIVERGENT-CONVERGENT-EVALUATIVE THINKING	FOLLOWING & CHANGING PLANS	IDENTIFYING PROBLEMS	MEETING DEADLINES	WORKING w/LIMITED RESOURCES	ACCEPTING RESPONSIBILITY	CONCENTRATION	CONTROLLING BEHAVIOR	FOLLOWING PROJECT OUTLINES	INDIVIDUALIZED STUDY HABITS	PERSISTENCE	SHARING SPACE	TAKING CARE OF MATERIALS	TIME MANAGEMENT	WORKING WITH OTHERS	PERSONAL MOTIVATION	SELF-AWARENESS	SENSE OF "QUALITY"	SETTING PERSONAL GOALS	CREATIVE EXPRESSION	CREATING STRATEGIES	DIORAMA & MODEL BUILDING	DRAWING & SKETCHING	POSTER MAKING	PUBLIC SPEAKING	SELF-CONFIDENCE	TEACHING OTHERS	WRITING
						X			X								0		X						X		X
						X			X								0		X						X		X
X			0	0	X	X	0	X	X	0		0			0	0	X	0	0	0					0	*	X
X			0	0	0	0	0	X		0			0		0	0	X	0	X	0			X		0	X	X
0			0	0	0	0	0	0	0	0			0		0	0	X	0	0				X		0		X
*	0		0	0	0	X	0	0	0	0			0		X	0	X	0	X	0		*	*	X	X		X
0	0				0	0	0	X		0			0		X	0	X	0	X	0		*	*	X	X		X
0			X	0	X	0	0	X	0	0	0	0	0		X	0	X	0	X	0				X			X
X	X	X	X	X	X	X	X	X	X	X	X	X	X	X	X	0	X	X	X	X	*	X	X	X	X	X	X
			X	0	X	0	0	X	X	0			X		X	0	X	0	X			*	*	*	0		X
0	0		X	0	X	0	0	X	X	X			X	X	X	0	X	0	X	0		*		*	0	X	X
X	0	X	X	0	X	X	X	X	X	X	0	0	X	*	X	0	X	X	X	0		*	*	*	X	0	X
X	0	X	X	0	X	X	X	X	X	X	0	0	X	*	X	0	X	X	X	0		*	*	*	X	0	X
X	0	X	X	0	X	X	X	X	X	X	0	0	X	*	X	0	X	X	X	0		*	*	*	X	0	X
X	0	X	X	0	X	X	X	X	X	X	0	0	X	*	X	0	X	X	X	0		*	*	*	X	0	X
X	X	X	#		#	X	#		#	X			X	X	#	X	X	X	X						X	*	X

Contents

Writing Project	Grade Level	Page

CONTENTS

THE PARTS OF SPEECH

Teacher Preview

Length of Project: 6 hours

Level of Independence: Basic

Goals:

1. To emphasize creative use of words.
2. To require the proper use of basic writing skills as students learn about the parts of speech.

During This Project Students Will:

1. Practice dictionary skills.
2. Use nouns, verbs, adjectives, and adverbs in sentences.
3. Read quotes from famous authors.
4. Identify parts of speech.

Skills:

Grammar	Concentration
Handwriting	Creative Expression
Neatness	Self-confidence
Sentences	Writing
Spelling	

Handouts Provided:

- "The Dictionary"
- "Quotes"
- "Word Substitution"

PROJECT CALENDAR:

HOUR 1: _____	HOUR 2: _____	HOUR 3: _____
Students are given "The Dictionary" handout. They look up words and create sentences.	Students continue to work on the handout.	"Quotes" handout is read and discussed, either as a class or in small groups.
HANDOUT PROVIDED NEED SPECIAL MATERIALS		HANDOUT PROVIDED
HOUR 4: _____	HOUR 5: _____	HOUR 6: _____
Students substitute their own words for certain words in the quotes on the "Word Substitution" handout.	Quotes from the handout are read in class, but with new words substituted by students.	Discussion of creative writing.
HANDOUT PROVIDED		
HOUR 7: _____	HOUR 8: _____	HOUR 9: _____

Lesson Plans and Notes

HOUR 1: Give students "The Dictionary" handout, which consists of a list of words. In class, the words are looked up one at a time by *all* students and the definitions are read orally. Discuss the part of speech for each word and ask students to invent sentences that use the word properly. After several sentences have been read for one word, the class decides which is best and students record this sentence on their handouts. Encourage (or require) all students to contribute to the discussion.

There are 31 words on the handout, which will require more than one hour to complete if time is allowed for students to discuss their sentences. A second hour is necessary (see Hour 2) and a third may be added to your project calendar if needed.

Notes:

- This project works best if every student has a dictionary to work with.
- Be sure that students know how to find which part of speech a word is by looking in a dictionary. It is important for them to understand that many words can be used in more than one way and that a word's position in a sentence usually determines what part of speech it is.
- The oral portion of this project can be reduced: students can look up definitions and write sentences on their own, rather than as a class. If this is done, the completion of "The Dictionary" can be made a homework assignment and Hour 2 can be a discussion of each student's work.

HOUR 2: The process begun in the first hour is continued until all 31 words are completed.

HOUR 3: Give students the handout "Quotes," which is a collection of quotes from the works of famous authors. Each quote contains at least one of the words on "The Dictionary" handout. The hour is spent reading the quotes and discussing how each author used nouns, verbs, adjectives, and adverbs. Have individual students read the quotes orally, either to the entire class or in small groups. Students may be required to identify what part of speech specific words represent, or answer questions like "How many adjectives can you find in this quote? What are they?"

Notes:

- The quotes on the second handout are drawn from classic literature and can be used in many ways. Each quote contains at least one word found on "The Dictionary": these words offer instructional possibilities for vocabulary and parts of speech. In addition to these words, other words in the quotes can be identified as nouns, verbs, adjectives, or adverbs (or other parts of speech if you wish to cover them). Time can be spent on sentence patterns and creative expression, and the quotes can be used to introduce students to a few classic authors.

HOUR 4: Give students the "Word Substitution" handout, which is actually an extension of "Quotes." The assignment calls for students to substitute new words for certain words in the quotes. For example, a typical question might be: "What word could you substitute for the word 'vaguely' in quote number one?" The new words may have meanings similar to the ones they replace, but this is not necessary. The only requirement for a new word is that it be the proper part of speech. Replacements for "vaguely" in the first quote might be "indifferently," "sillily," "dimly," "stupidly," or "daringly." Of course, there are many others as well.

Students work on this handout for the entire hour, making constant use of their dictionaries. If the handouts cannot be completed in one hour they become homework assignments. Also, if synonyms are to be emphasized, this is an opportunity to introduce students to the use of a thesaurus.

HOUR 5: Students bring their completed handouts to class. The hour is spent reading the "new" quotations made with substitute words. Emphasis is placed on the parts of speech and whether or not the words chosen by students are grammatically appropriate replacements for the words that were removed.

HOUR 6: Use this hour for a discussion of creative writing. Why is it important to know the parts of speech and to recognize how they are used in sentences? How does a writer benefit from developing a good vocabulary? What does a project like this offer students who want to learn on their own? Students may be asked to bring in excerpts from stories they have read, or they may be asked to write one-paragraph descriptions of settings or characters that are assigned in class.

Name _____ Date _____

THE DICTIONARY
Student Assignment Sheet

Writing is an extremely important communication skill. A person who writes well has the ability to express ideas, opinions and descriptions; this is a valuable asset in school and in most careers. Being able to write will give you an advantage in a competitive world. Although it isn't often mentioned, people *are* impressed by someone who has command of the English language, uses words correctly, and writes clearly and to the point. Gaining command of writing skills is also necessary for learning on your own because information must be recorded, organized, and put into final form before it can be used. Look upon projects like this as steps toward increasing your vocabulary and improving your creative writing skills.

ASSIGNMENT:
    Look up the words listed below in the dictionary and write a good sentence for each. Label each word as a noun, verb, adjective, or adverb. If a word can be used in more than one way, choose *one,* and write a sentence using the word correctly.

Word	Part of Speech	Sentence
1. Vaguely	_____	_____
2. Prudently	_____	_____
3. Wistful	_____	_____
4. Fervent	_____	_____
5. Disquieting	_____	_____

6. Gesture   _____   _____

7. Blithe   _____   _____

8. Jocund   _____   _____

9. Congeal   _____   _____

10. Presume   _____   _____

11. Intellect   _____   _____

12. Apprehensive _____   _____

13. Furrow   _____   _____

14. Mallet   _____   _____

15. Curious   _____   _____

16. Tread   _____   _____

17. Strenuously   _____   _____

18. Countenance _____   _____

19. Tranquil   _____   _____

20. Convulsion _____ _____
                                     _____

21. Perpetually _____ _____
                                     _____

22. Noisily _____ _____
                                 _____

23. Dreadfully _____ _____
                                    _____

24. Scoff _____ _____
                               _____

25. Apparition _____ _____
                                    _____

26. Glade _____ _____
                               _____

27. Portent _____ _____
                                 _____

28. Furtively _____ _____
                                   _____

29. Excruciating _____ _____
                                      _____

30. Disgruntled _____ _____
                                     _____

31. Abet _____ _____
                              _____

QUOTES
Student Assignment Sheet

LEARN FROM THE MASTERS

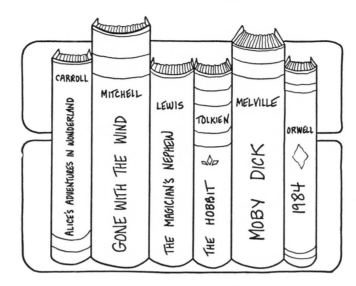

One of the best ways to see how words can be used is too read the works of great authors. They are considered "great" because they know how to use words creatively to give the reader a clear mental image of something. Below are short quotes taken from the works of some of the most famous authors in the world. As you read, think about their choice of words and how such words add impact, clarity, or "color" to the thoughts being expressed. Also, consider the possibility of picking up a book by one of these authors to read for yourself. Some of them may be a bit too difficult for you to read now, but it won't be long before you will be able to read any of them with pleasure and understanding.

1. "The street was a blind alley. Winston halted, stood for several seconds wondering <u>vaguely</u> what to do, then turned round and began to retrace his steps."
   1984, by George Orwell

2. "The hermit cast a <u>wistful</u> look upon the knight, in which there was a sort of comic expression of hesitation, as if uncertain how far he should act <u>prudently</u> in trusting his guest."
   Ivanhoe, by Sir Walter Scott

3. "Despite his <u>fervent</u> prayers, however, he remained a prisoner."
   The Count of Monte Cristo, by Alexandre Dumas

4. "At times they heard <u>disquieting</u> laughter. Sometimes there was singing in the distance too."
   The Hobbit, by J.R.R. Tolkien

5. "With a <u>gesture</u> both simple and majestic, Jehan opened the purse before the captain's eyes."
   The Hunchback of Notre Dame, by Victor Hugo

6. "And now a thousand kinds of little painted birds began to warble in the trees, and with their <u>blithe</u> and <u>jocund</u> notes seemed to welcome and salute the fresh dawn...."
   Don Quixote, by Cervantes

7. "...Ahab for hours and hours would stand gazing dead to windward, while an occasional squall of sleet or snow would all but <u>congeal</u> his very eyelashes together."
   Moby Dick, by Herman Melville

8. "A boy, <u>presuming</u> on his <u>intellect</u>,
   Once showed two little monkeys in a cage
   A burning-glass they could not understand
   And never could understand."
   "At Woodward's Gardens," by Robert Frost

9. "The Natives came by Degrees to be <u>apprehensive</u> of any Danger from me. I would sometimes lie down, and let five or six of them dance on my hand."
   Gulliver's Travels, by Jonathan Swift

10. "Alice thought she had never seen such a curious croquet-ground in her life: it was all ridges and <u>furrows</u>: the croquet balls were live hedgehogs, and the <u>mallets</u> live flamingoes..."
    Alice's Adventures in Wonderland, by Lewis Carroll

11. "As he ran with his comrades he <u>strenuously</u> tried to think, but all he knew was that if he fell down those coming behind would <u>tread</u> upon him."
    The Red Badge of Courage, by Stephen Crane

12. "...and I noticed that he was fat and baldheaded, and had an expression of winning gentleness and simplicity upon his <u>tranquil</u> <u>countenance</u>."
    "The Notorious Jumping Frog of Calaveras County," by Mark Twain

13. "With a <u>convulsion</u> of the mind, Ralph discovered dirt and decay, understood how much he disliked <u>perpetually</u> flicking the tangled hair out of his eyes, and at last, when the sun was gone, rolling <u>noisily</u> to rest among the dry leaves."
    Lord of the Flies, by William Golding

14. "It was <u>dreadfully</u> unlike anything a grown-up would be expected to do."
    The Magician's Nephew, by C.S. Lewis

15. "And these shelves were loaded with little articles, soap and talcum powder, razors and those Western magazines ranch men love to read and <u>scoff</u> at and secretly believe."
    Of Mice and Men, by John Steinbeck

16. "What the waiter thought of such a strange little <u>apparition</u> coming in all alone, I don't know..."
    David Copperfield, by Charles Dickens

17. "Then the plane was overhead, its shadow passing over the open <u>glade</u>, the throbbing reaching its maximum <u>portent</u>."
    For Whom the Bell Tolls, by Ernest Hemingway

18. "He looked up <u>furtively</u> as she entered. The pain of moving his eyes was too <u>excruciating</u> to be borne and he groaned."
    Gone With the Wind, by Margaret Mitchell

19. "Princess Marya, sitting in the drawing room and listening to the <u>disgruntled</u> talk of the old men, understood nothing of what she was hearing."
    War and Peace, by Leo Tolstoy

20. "The elements, however, <u>abetted</u> me in making a path through the deepest snow in the woods..."
    Walden, by Henry David Thoreau

WORD SUBSTITUTION
Student Assignment Sheet

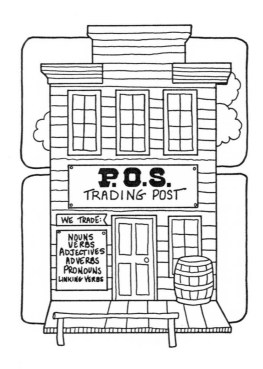

Building a solid, useful vocabulary is an important process for the serious writer. Quite often the choice of a word can make the difference between a clearly stated thought and a confused statement, between a creative description and an unimaginative one. Use the dictionary for this project, and try to find colorful, descriptive, and unusual words that will help increase your vocabulary.

    The words below come from the "Quotes" handout. This list includes some words that are not underlined on that handout. Think of two substitutes for each word. Your words need not have the same meaning as the ones they replace; they must, however, be the same part of speech. Replace an adjective with an adjective, for example, even if the meanings are totally different. The first word is done for you to illustrate how this handout is to be completed.

Word	Quote	Part of Speech	Substitute 1	Substitute 2
1. vaguely	1	adverb	stupidly	daringly
2. blind	1			
3. wistful	2			
4. comic	2			
5. prudently	2			
6. fervent	3			

7. prayers	3		
8. prisoner	3		
9. disquieting	4		
10. laughter	4		
11. singing	4		
12. gesture	5		
13. majestic	5		
14. purse	5		
15. painted	6		
16. warble	6		
17. blithe	6		
18. jocund	6		
19. occasional	7		
20. squall	7		
21. congeal	7		
22. presuming	8		
23. intellect	8		
24. natives	9		
25. apprehensive	9		
26. curious	10		
27. croquet-ground	10		
28. furrows	10		
29. comrades	11		
30. strenuously	11		
31. tread	11		
32. fat	12		
33. winning	12		
34. tranquil	12		

35. countenance	12			
36. convulsion	13			
37. perpetually	13			
38. flicking	13			
39. noisily	13			
40. dreadfully	14			
41. grown-up	14			
42. loaded	15			
43. scoff	15			
44. waiter	16			
45. apparition	16			
46. glade	17			
47. throbbing	17			
48. maximum	17			
49. portent	17			
50. furtively	18			
51. eyes	18			
52. excruciating	18			
53. borne	18			
54. groaned	18			
55. sitting	19			
56. disgruntled	19			
57. elements	20			
58. abetted	20			
59. deepest	20			
60. woods	20			

IMAGINARY WORDS

Teacher Preview

Length of Project: 2 hours

Level of Independence: Basic

Goals:

1. To emphasize creative use of words.
2. To require the proper use of writing skills as students learn about the parts of speech.

During This Project Students Will:

1. Use nouns, verbs, adjectives, and adverbs in sentences.
2. Identify nouns, verbs, adjectives, and adverbs by their positions in sentences.

Skills:

Grammar	Concentration
Neatness	Creative Expression
Sentences	Self-confidence
Spelling	Writing
Handwriting	

Handouts Provided:

- "Student Assignment Sheet"

PROJECT CALENDAR:

HOUR 1: _____	HOUR 2: _____	HOUR 3: _____
Students are given assignment sheets and the hour is spent working on them.	Discussion of the assignment; students read their sentences to the class.	
HANDOUT PROVIDED	STUDENTS TURN IN WORK	
HOUR 4: _____	**HOUR 5:** _____	**HOUR 6:** _____
HOUR 7: _____	**HOUR 8:** _____	**HOUR 9:** _____

Lesson Plans and Notes

HOUR 1: Give students the "Imaginary Words" Assignment Sheet. Spend the first part of the hour explaining the project; the remaining time is used by students to work on the handout. Since handouts will probably not be completed by the end of the hour, they become homework assignments.

Notes:

- This project is based upon the fact that words appear in certain patterns in sentences. If these patterns are understood, it is possible to tell what part of speech a word is, even if you don't know the word or if the word is imaginary or "made up."

- The handout for this project does not discuss sentence patterns. It is assumed that students know about the parts of speech and where each part is typically positioned in properly constructed sentences. Most students can intuitively substitute real words for imaginary ones even if they know little about sentence patterns.

- Students can be required to write out each sentence with the "real" words they list on their handouts. This should be done on notebook paper.

- "Imaginary Words" can be made into a "dictionary search" project. Supply students with dictionaries and tell them to *find* replacement words. Remind them that many adjectives become adverbs by adding "-ly" *but* not all adverbs end in "-ly."

HOUR 2: Completed assignments are brought to class and discussed. Assignments are collected at the end of the hour.

Note:

- To extend this project, have students invent their own imaginary words and create imaginary sentences.

Name _____ Date _____

IMAGINARY WORDS
Student Assignment Sheet

You should be able to tell if a word is a noun, a verb, an adjective, or an adverb by looking at its position in a sentence and at the other words around it. You can usually do this even if you don't know the word, or if the word is an imaginary, nonsensical word.

    Below is a series of imaginary sentences. Each sentence has two or more imaginary words in it. In Section Two, tell what part of speech each imaginary word represents, then think of *two* real words that could replace it in the sentence. The first one is done for you as an example.

SECTION ONE: Imaginary Sentences

1. The <u>pibnox</u> hit the <u>flin</u>.

2. I understand the <u>stoom</u> looks <u>yabble</u>.

3. The <u>wickside</u> drove his <u>bulnar</u> <u>dakely</u>.

4. Where did <u>Num</u> get that <u>slive</u> <u>clacker</u>?

5. This <u>ornip</u> is <u>plub</u>.

6. This <u>zeeker</u> is a <u>pitstern</u>.

7. He ran <u>huffblind</u> until his body <u>splunged</u>.

8. She loved her <u>snoof</u>, so she punished him <u>biffly</u>.

9. The <u>evanstark</u> carried his <u>blommer</u> all the way to the <u>mainskip</u>.

10. The <u>hostner</u> was <u>oddsman</u> even though he <u>vibbed</u> the <u>glurch</u>.

11. Why don't you put your <u>lupey</u> bike in a <u>mandex</u> where it will be <u>quist</u>?

12. <u>Slod</u> ran <u>tramfitly</u> toward the <u>glumpcar</u>, with his <u>zycop</u> trailing behind in the dust.

13. The <u>simstod</u> shouted <u>flarishly</u> into the <u>triphaze</u> <u>gamblight</u>.

14. Mary <u>higgled</u> her <u>beele</u> <u>jubely</u> until it <u>splonched</u> and everyone saw it <u>gliping</u>.

15. They had never seen a <u>nobber</u> act so <u>ravinly</u> or so <u>speenly</u>; it was a <u>floran</u> <u>nobber</u>, though, so its <u>pixen</u> behavior was quite <u>trapid</u>. Still, they wished it would <u>hobert</u> and not <u>plouster</u> any more.

IMAGINARY WORDS (continued)

SECTION TWO

Imaginary Word	Part of Speech	Replacement 1	Replacement 2
1. pibnox	noun	car	boy
flin	noun	tree	ball
2. stoom			
yabble			
3. wickside			
bulnar			
dakely			
4. Num			
slive			
clacker			
5. ornip			
plub			
6. zeeker			
pitstern			
7. huffblind			
splunged			
8. snoof			
biffly			
9. evanstark			
blommer			
mainskip			
10. hostner			
oddsman			
vibbed			
glurch			

17

Imaginary Word	Part of Speech	Replacement 1	Replacement 2
11. lupey	——————	——————————	——————————
mandex	——————	——————————	——————————
quist	——————	——————————	——————————
12. Slod	——————	——————————	——————————
tramfitly	——————	——————————	——————————
glumpcar	——————	——————————	——————————
zycop	——————	——————————	——————————
13. simstod	——————	——————————	——————————
flarishly	——————	——————————	——————————
triphaze	——————	——————————	——————————
gamblight	——————	——————————	——————————
14. higgled	——————	——————————	——————————
beele	——————	——————————	——————————
jubely	——————	——————————	——————————
splonched	——————	——————————	——————————
gliping	——————	——————————	——————————
15. nobber	——————	——————————	——————————
ravinly	——————	——————————	——————————
speenly	——————	——————————	——————————
floran	——————	——————————	——————————
pixen	——————	——————————	——————————
trapid	——————	——————————	——————————
hobert	——————	——————————	——————————
plouster	——————	——————————	——————————

WRITING REPORTS

Teacher Preview

General Explanation:

The purpose of this project is to require students to use the "Five S's," (five steps for preparing to write a report) as they embark on simple research assignments. The "Five S's" are

1. Survey
2. Specialize
3. Study
4. Summarize
5. Structure

These five steps are explained in the "Information Sheet for the Five S's."

Length of Project: 5 hours

Level of Independence: Basic

Goals:

1. To supply students with an understanding of how to produce a written report.
2. To prepare students for future projects that require written reports.
3. To require the proper use of writing skills.

During This Project Students Will:

1. Practice basic writing skills.
2. Practice basic research skills.
3. Assemble information for reports.
4. Prepare proper bibliographies.
5. Write correct outlines.
6. Write well-organized reports.

Skills:

Preparing bibliographies	Organizing
Collecting data	Outlining
Summarizing	Selecting topics
Grammar	Divergent-convergent-evaluative thinking

19

Handwriting   Following project outlines
Neatness   Accepting responsibility
Paragraphs   Writing
Sentences   Individualized study habits
Spelling   Sense of "quality"
Concentration

Handouts Provided:

- "Information Sheet for the Five S's"
- "Writing Reports, Student Assignment Sheet 1"
- "Writing Reports, Student Assignment Sheet 2"
- Student Research Guide (optional; see Appendix)
    - a. "Bibliographies"
    - b. "Notecards and Bibliographies"

PROJECT CALENDAR:

HOUR 1: _____	**HOUR 2:** _____	**HOUR 3:** _____
Students are given an informational handout. The hour is spent discussing the five S's: survey, specialize, study, summarize, structure.	After choosing general subject areas, students survey newspapers for articles. The first assignment sheet is used and short reports are written.	Review work from Hour 2. Using the second assignment sheet and the five S's, students begin work on individual reports. All students work with the same general subject (chosen by the teacher).
HANDOUT PROVIDED PREPARATION REQUIRED	HANDOUT PROVIDED NEED SPECIAL MATERIALS STUDENTS TURN IN WORK	HANDOUT PROVIDED RETURN STUDENT WORK PREPARATION REQUIRED
HOUR 4: _____	**HOUR 5:** _____	**HOUR 6:** _____
Students continue to collect information and work on reports.	Outlines, bibliographies and written reports are turned in. Discussion of how the ability to write reports benefits independent learners.	
	STUDENTS TURN IN WORK	
HOUR 7: _____	**HOUR 8:** _____	**HOUR 9:** _____

Lesson Plans and Notes

HOUR 1: Give students the information sheet and discuss each of the five steps. Take the class through the process of writing a report, one step at a time. For example, say to the class: "Using 'astronomy' as our subject, I will demonstrate how to conduct a survey, choose a topic in which to specialize, find material to study, summarize important findings, and structure facts into an outline. I want you to copy this outline as I put it on the board."

The Five S's: Outline for Astronomy

I.   SURVEY: Look up "astronomy" or "space" in two or three encyclopedias and record possible topics such as the following:
  A. Planets
  B. Sun
  C. Moon
  D. Quasars
  E. Black holes
  F. Astronomers
  G. Light
  H. Constellations
  I. Galaxies

II. SPECIALIZE: Choose the topic that most interests you. For this example we will choose the sun.

III. STUDY: Read and learn as much as you can about the sun.

IV. SUMMARIZE: Using your own words list the important facts you have discovered about the sun.
  A. The sun is about 93 million miles away from the earth.
  B. Light from the sun takes about 6 minutes to get here.
  C. The sun loses mass at the rate of about 4 million metric tons per second.
  D. All of the energy we use on earth (except atomic energy) began with the sun.
  E. The sun's energy comes from hydrogen atoms that turn into helium atoms (fusion reaction).

V.   STRUCTURE: Organize these facts into outline form so that they are ready to be written into a report.

Notes:

• Some preparation work is necessary for this first hour: have two or three different encyclopedia articles about astronomy or space on hand when work on the outline begins. Read parts of the articles to students and actually *show* them how to conduct a survey of topics.

- Expand the brief outline provided for this hour as much as possible. Add topics to the survey and facts to the summary of information.

- In addition to general information about astronomy, have several books and magazine articles that are specifically about the sun. Show students where specific facts were found. Read passages to them and discuss as a class how to summarize what is read. Also emphasize the use of bibliographies.

- When a list of 15 or 20 summarized facts has been developed, discuss with the class how these should be structured (or organized) to make a report. Make an outline that clearly shows where paragraphs will begin and end.

- Students' notes from this hour may be collected and checked.

HOUR 2: You will need newspapers from the past two or three weeks for this activity, at least two or three issues per student. Begin the hour by presenting students with a list of possible subjects to choose from, and hand out "Writing Reports, Student Assignment Sheet 1." These are subjects that can be found in a newspaper:

Economics and business	Science
Politics	Sports
Accidents and disasters	Education
Government	International news
Fashion	National news
Entertainment	State news
Opinion	Local news
Strange happenings and oddities	Crime

Each student chooses one subject and then conducts a survey of at least three newspapers for headlines that fit within the scope of the subject. Students then follow the assignment sheet to produce outlines and two- or three-paragraph reports. Allow students to clip articles and trade papers so they have access to more resources. Scissors will be needed. Students turn their work in at the end of the hour unless you assign it as homework.

HOUR 3: Return student work from Hour 2 and discuss any problems that were encountered. For this hour you must choose one subject and provide as much resource material as possible about it. You might choose a subject from the following list:

Astronomy	Automobiles	Insects
Weather	Travel	Airplanes
Indians	Your home state	The oceans

Animals	Famous people	Rocks and minerals
The arts	Plants	History

This subject (whatever you choose) is assigned to every student and each must conduct a survey, select a topic, study it, summarize a few pertinent facts, structure them appropriately, and write a brief report. Students use "Writing Reports, Student Assignment Sheet 2" as a guide. This work continues during Hour 4.

It is crucial that plenty of resource material be available to students. Choose the subject carefully several weeks before this activity is presented, and begin collecting books, magazines, articles, clippings and other materials. Contact the school librarian (or a local public library) and make arrangements for a special one-week loan of an entire "mini-library" about the subject. Send a note home with students and ask for loans of encyclopedias, books and magazines. If plenty of resources are on hand this activity works well.

HOUR 4: Students continue to collect information and work on written reports.

HOUR 5: Students hand in their outlines, written reports (two to three pages) and bibliographies. Spend the rest of the hour discussing the importance of the skills presented in this project. Why is it necessary for students to learn how to write reports? What careers require people to be able to record information in report form? Are such skills used in high school and college? How does the ability to write a report help a student become an independent learner? Strong emphasis should be placed on careers that require report writing. Some professionals who must frequently prepare reports are:

Lawyers	Military personnel
Doctors	Educators
Engineers	Historians
Politicians	Scientists
Government workers	Technicians
Secretaries	Business people
Urban planners	Police officers
Architects	News reporters

Encourage students to interview adults in various professions to find out for themselves the importance of gathering information and writing reports.

Note:

• Try to incorporate the five steps for preparing to write a report into other areas of the curriculum. Require students to go through the five steps whenever they write reports or conduct research projects.

INFORMATION SHEET FOR THE FIVE S's

One of the important requirements made of students as they become more independent in their schoolwork is the ability to write reports. Reports are a method of showing others what has been learned. In school, reports sometimes take the place of tests; in high school and college they are often required as final course projects. The ability to write a good report can actually open up more learning opportunities. A properly written report is *proof* that the writer has command of necessary learning skills and is capable of studying areas of interest independently.

This handout explains five steps for producing a written report.

1. SURVEY. Before choosing a topic take time to survey the field and carefully decide which topics would make a good project. Encyclopedias are great for this. For example, if the subject you are studying is astronomy, the field is huge: planets, sun, moon, quazars, black holes, astronomers, light, constellations, galaxies, and so forth. Make a list of topics that interest you.

2. SPECIALIZE. After you survey the subject area, narrow the selections down to one topic that is particularly appealing. This becomes your report topic. For example, suppose you are very interested in the sun and you found a lot of solid information during your survey for astronomy—you may decide to *specialize* by studying the sun.

3. STUDY. Once a topic is chosen you can be much more specific about resource material. During your survey you looked up "astronomy" and found general information about the sun, along with many other topics. Now you can look up "sun" and find more detailed information and many more facts. Study the topic until you understand some things about it: *learn* about it by reading, watching, asking, and listening.

4. SUMMARIZE. As you study, record information so that it can be used in a report. This information should be *summarized* in an outline or on notecards. Obviously you cannot record everything you find since you will undoubtedly find many books about the sun. Be selective; when you find useful information, record it briefly in your own words.

5. STRUCTURE. When you are through studying, and have summarized the information, you are ready to organize it into logical order so that it can be written into a report. Structuring has three steps:

   a. Organize your notecards, if you used them. The great advantage of notecards is that they can be arranged and rearranged. Work with them until you are comfortable with the arrangement of facts, ideas, theories, opinions, events, and conclusions.

   b. Make an outline. Once the facts you wish to present are laid out in order, outline all of the major headings and subheadings (or topics and subtopics) in the exact order that you want to write about them. Each major heading should represent the beginning of a new paragraph.

   c. Write your report. Each paragraph should contain a central idea, and the flow of the paragraphs through the report should be smooth and logical. Of course, spelling, grammar, punctuation, capitalization, and sentence structure must be correct, and the report must be done in your neatest handwriting. Remember, *a bibliography is required.*

Name _____ Date _____

WRITING REPORTS
Student Assignment Sheet 1

This assignment is a "mini-research" exercise that allows you to become familiar with the five steps described on the information sheet. Choose a subject from the list provided by the teacher, then follow the five S's:

Step 1:
SURVEY

Survey several newspapers for articles about your subject and list at least ten headlines that are related to it in some way.

Step 2:
SPECIALIZE

Identify a specific topic that is covered in at least two of the articles.

Step 3:
STUDY

Read these two articles and underline important facts.

Step 4:
SUMMARIZE

Summarize ten of the facts you have underlined.

Step 5:
STRUCTURE

Write a two- to three-paragraph report about the topic you have studied.

To complete your assignment:

FIRST: On notebook paper, record your subject, the ten headlines, the topic you chose, ten summarized facts, and a final arrangement of facts into an outline that looks like this:

I. Subject: <u>(Choose one from your teacher's list.)</u> _____
    A. Headline 1
    B. Headline 2
    C. Headline 3
    D. Etc. (Record at least ten headlines)

II. Topic for study: <u>(At least two of the headlines must apply specifically to it.)</u>

III. Summary of facts (about the topic)
    A. Fact 1
    B. Fact 2
    C. Fact 3
    D. Etc. (Record at least ten facts)

IV. Facts arranged into the best order for a report
    A. (Arrange the facts so that they fit together into several **paragraphs**).
    B. Etc.

SECOND: Write a two- to three-paragraph report from your final outline of facts. Group related facts together into paragraphs. Decide what order the paragraphs should be in and think of a way to blend the facts into a smooth flow of ideas rather than short, disjointed sentences. Finally, check over your written report to be sure it makes sense.

THIRD: Hand in your outline and report. The outline will be graded for neatness and proper construction; the report will be graded for writing skills and how well it presents information.

© 1987 by The Center for Applied Research in Education, Inc.

Name _____ Date _____

WRITING REPORTS
Student Assignment Sheet 2

This assignment is similar to the first, only it is more thorough and will require more time. Your teacher has chosen a subject for everyone in the class to study and you will again practice the five steps for preparing a report by studying topics that relate to the subject. Here is the assignment outline:

SURVEY   I.   Survey books, magazines and other materials that are provided around the classroom and find at least ten topics that you might like to study. Everyone's topic will relate to the same subject area.

SPECIALIZE   II.   From this list of ten choose *one* topic.

STUDY   III.   Find at least twenty facts about the topic.

SUMMARIZE   IV.   Record the facts in your own words.

STRUCTURE   V.   Prepare an outline and write a two- to three-page report.

To complete your assignment:

FIRST: On notebook paper, record the subject, list the topics found during your survey and record your topic choice. Then, list your summarized facts and make a final arrangement of facts into an outline that looks like this:

     I.   Subject: (This is determined by the teacher.) _____

       A.   Topic 1

       B.   Topic 2

       C.   Topic 3

       D.   Etc. (Find and record at least ten topics)

     II.   Topic for study: (Choose one from the above list.) _____

     III.   Summary of facts

       A.   Fact 1

       B.   Fact 2

       C.   Fact 3

       D.   Etc. (Record at least twenty facts)

     IV.   Facts arranged into the best order for a report. Group them according to paragraphs. For example:

       A.   Paragraph 1

         1. Fact 6   *Write the facts out!*

         2. Fact 13

         3. Fact 17

       B.   Paragraph 2

         1. Fact 2

         2. Fact 18

         3. Etc.

       C.   Paragraph 3

       D.   Etc.

SECOND: Write a two- to three-page report about the topic from your final list of facts. This report must include a bibliography.

THIRD: Hand in your outline and report. The outline will be graded for neatness and proper construction; the report will be graded for writing skills and how well it presents information. The bibliography will also receive a grade.

Note: This project did not require the use of notecards, but their value should be obvious. Notecards allow you to arrange and rearrange facts in any way that pleases you. This is extremely helpful when working with large numbers of facts.

WRITING ESSAYS

Teacher Preview

Length of Project: 4 hours

Level of Independence: Basic

Goals:

1. To emphasize basic writing skills.
2. To encourage creative self-expression.

During This Project Students Will:

1. Discuss topics for essays.
2. Assemble information for an essay.
3. Take careful notes during class discussion.
4. Formulate opinions about a specific subject.
5. Produce correct outlines.
6. Write well-organized essays.

Skills:

Collecting Data	Organizing
Interviewing	Outlining
Listening	Selecting topics
Summarizing	Divergent-convergent-evaluative thinking
Grammar	Following project outlines
Handwriting	Sense of "quality"
Neatness	Creative expression
Paragraphs	Teaching others
Sentences	Public speaking
Spelling	Writing

Handouts Provided:

- "Student Assignment Sheet"

PROJECT CALENDAR:

HOUR 1: _____	**HOUR 2:** _____	**HOUR 3:** _____
Introduction to the term "essay" and discussion of the assignment. Students choose a topic for the class to write essays about. HANDOUT PROVIDED	Students bring facts about the essay topic to class; everyone takes notes during a discussion of these facts. Students are encouraged to find additional information for Hour 3.	Students outline essays that describe personal points of view and hand them in at the end of the hour. _Return graded outlines between Hours 3 and 4 so students can write their essays at home._ STUDENTS TURN IN WORK
HOUR 4: _____	**HOUR 5:** _____	**HOUR 6:** _____
Finished essays are read to the class and handed in. STUDENTS TURN IN WORK		
HOUR 7: _____	**HOUR 8:** _____	**HOUR 9:** _____

Lesson Plans and Notes

HOUR 1: Introduce students to the term "essay." They should understand that an essay is an "analytic, interpretive, or critical literary composition…usually dealing with its subject from a limited often personal point of view." *(Webster's Third New International Dictionary)*

Explain to the students that an essay supports or puts forth an opinion by using facts, solid arguments, and accurate information. With this in mind, spend the remaining portion of the hour selecting a topic for everyone in the class to write an essay about. After discussing a number of topics from the list below, students select one by vote. This becomes the "class topic." As a class, narrow the scope of the topic and specify what kinds of resources are available. An additional hour may be included if a more thorough discussion is desired.

At the end of this hour give students the assignment sheet. Each student is to find two facts or pieces of information about the chosen topic and record them in writing. These pieces of information are brought to class for the next hour.

ESSAY TOPICS

Drunk driving	Education
Child abuse	Smoking
Unemployment	America's role in the Middle East
Student rights	The president of the United States
Genetic engineering	The welfare system
Computers	Democracy
The space program	Environmental pollution
The arms race	Spies and traitors in America
Modern music	Drug abuse
The American "infrastructure"	Terrorism
Railroads	Divorce and split families
Euthanasia	Immigration
The future	World population
The Equal Rights Amendment	State issues
Free enterprise	Local issues
Communism	School issues

Notes:

• This project offers an opportunity to emphasize the use of the Five S's: survey, specialize, study, summarize and structure (see project W-3: "Writing Reports").

- Expand this project by reading several essays in class to help students understand the essay style and form. Provide an extra hour if readings are to be included in the project. Examples of essays can be found in the editorials of any daily newspaper. In addition, there are essay collections available in book form in libraries and bookstores.

HOUR 2: Students bring their written facts to class for discussion. Each student reads his or her information to the class; everyone is required to take notes on information as it is presented. At the end of the hour students should have a set of facts that can be used in their essays. Tell students that their assignment for the next hour is to decide upon a specific point of view to express. Encourage them to find additional information to use in their essays and to record this data in the notes that they bring to class for Hour 3.

HOUR 3: Students come to class prepared with notes from the second hour, personal points of view about the topic, and any additional information that they have collected. This hour is spent outlining the essays. Each student arranges his or her facts into a logical order. This outline should clearly show what information will be included in each paragraph of the essay. Outlining is done in class so that help can be offered to students as they organize their material. Student outlines should be handed in, either at the end of the hour or the following day. When you return the graded outlines, tell the students to write their essays at home and bring them to class for the fourth hour when they will be read to the class. Be sure they know when the due date is.

HOUR 4: Students read their essays to the class and then hand them in to be graded. More than one hour may be needed for all essays to be read especially if they are discussed afterwards in class. Require that poorly written essays be redone.

Notes:

- It is not necessary to have students read their essays in class. Oral reading helps bring up discussion topics and allows immediate critical analysis of each student's work, but it is time consuming. Alternatives are to have students read their essays to each other in small groups or to simply have them hand in their written work.

- After essays are handed in, it is a good idea to devote some time to a discussion of the importance of building essay-writing skills. This discussion should center on future needs (essay tests, careers) and the value of being able to state an opinion and support it with facts and logical arguments. If these things are discussed during Hour 1, they can be reinforced here.

General Notes About This Project:

- This can be made into a much more challenging project by requiring each student to select his or her own topic. This transforms the project into a research project and yields a greater diversity of writings.

- Another suggestion is to use this project *twice,* once when the entire class works together on one topic, and again when each student chooses a different topic.

- One more variation: use only one topic for the class, but require each student to find enough facts independently to write an essay. You can then have an excellent discussion based on each student's research (30 students with 20 facts each equals 600 facts!). Allow at least one week for research if you organize the project this way.

WRITING ESSAYS
Student Assignment Sheet

Writing an essay is like writing a report, only in an essay the author has the freedom to express a personal point of view. To be effective, an essay should be factual and carefully organized so that the reader can understand the point being made and also take the work seriously. Essays are written for many reasons. They appear in the editorial sections of daily newspapers, and most news magazines reserve space each week for commentators to write about current issues. Some people write essays without ever having them published, just to record their opinions. In school, especially in college, students are asked to write essays to illustrate their understanding of certain subjects. The ability to write a good essay will come in handy in the future. Anyone who is serious about learning independently should develop the skills for producing brief, well-written papers about subjects of importance or personal interest.

For this project you will write an essay by deciding upon a specific point that you want to make—or opinion that you would like to express—and collecting facts to help support what you write. Here is the assignment:

I. As a class, choose a subject to write essays about from a list that your teacher will provide.

II. Find at least two interesting facts or pieces of information about the subject the class has chosen. These facts can come from books, magazines, television, newspapers, adult experts, or any other source of accurate information. Remember: your information must be accurate!

III. Write down the facts you find and bring them to class to share with everyone else. During class discussion take notes on the information that is presented by other students.

IV. Formulate an opinion about the subject after hearing and recording information from the class discussion. You may gather more facts to support your opinion if you wish.

V. After collecting additional facts, come to class prepared to outline your essay. This outline will be handed in so the teacher can be sure your essay is well planned.

VI. When your outline is returned, write the essay. Be as neat as possible and strive for quality. Try to convince others that your opinion or point of view is worth listening to and that you know what you are talking about.

VII. Read your essay to the class and then hand it in to be graded.

WRITING LETTERS

Teacher Preview

General Explanation:

Students write several letters for this project but none of them are actually mailed. "Writing Letters" requires students to decide who would be the best person to write to about a specific situation or concern. All the people and addresses provided on the assignment sheet, however, are fictitious.

Length of Project: 4 hours

Level of Independence: Basic

Goals:

1. To supply students with an understanding of how to write letters for a variety of purposes.
2. To prepare students for future projects that require letter writing.
3. To require the proper use of letterwriting skills.

During This Project Students Will:

1. Prepare well-organized business letters.

Skills:

Writing letters	Spelling
Grammar	Organizing
Handwriting	Outlining
Neatness	Public speaking
Paragraphs	Sense of "quality"
Sentences	Writing

Handouts Provided:

- "Student Assignment Sheet"
- Student Research Guide (see Appendix)
  a. "Sending for Information"
     "Example of the Block Letter Style"
     "Example of a Modified Block Letter Style"

PROJECT CALENDAR:

HOUR 1: _____	HOUR 2: _____	HOUR 3: _____
Students write letters, based upon instructions given in class.	Graded letters from Hour 1 are returned and common mistakes are discussed. A second letter is assigned as homework.	Students read their letters to each other in small groups. A third letter is assigned as homework.
HANDOUTS PROVIDED STUDENTS TURN IN WORK	RETURN STUDENT WORK	STUDENTS TURN IN WORK
HOUR 4: _____	HOUR 5: _____	HOUR 6: _____
Graded letters from Hour 3 are returned. Students read their homework assignments for Hour 4 in small groups. Brief full-class discussion of the value of letter writing.		
RETURN STUDENT WORK STUDENTS TURN IN WORK		
HOUR 7: _____	HOUR 8: _____	HOUR 9: _____

Lesson Plans and Notes

HOUR 1: Give students the assignment sheet containing a set of fictitious names and addresses, along with additional information about each "person" listed. Then read a "situation" to the class and have each student decide upon a person (from the assignment sheet) to write a letter to. Each student then writes his or her letter and hands it in at the end of the hour.

Here are three possible "situations" that may be read to students at the beginning of this hour:

1. You have noticed that the family next door is mistreating its pets by keeping them in tiny pens and not feeding and watering them properly. The animals are sick, and it makes you angry to see them so mistreated. You decide to take action by writing a letter.

2. You have been given an assignment to do a research project on endangered animals and have decided to study snow leopards. Upon looking further into the problems of endangered animals, you become very concerned for their safety and continued existence. You decide to write a letter to someone who can not only provide some information about snow leopards but can also actually do something about protecting endangered animals. You want to ask for information *and* state an opinion.

3. During the summer you found a turtle that you want to keep as a pet. Having no idea how to take care of it and not even knowing what kind of turtle it is, you decide to take a photograph and send it, along with a request for help, to someone who should know about taking care of animals.

Notes:

• The scope of this project can be expanded by creating additional "situations" and new "people" for the student handout. The emphasis in the material provided is placed on animals. You may want to emphasize science or child abuse or politics or current events or business or any of many other potential topics.

• Models for "block" and "modified block" letter styles can be found in the Student Research Guide ("Sending for Information" handout). They should be given to students during this hour, to serve as examples.

HOUR 2: Return the students' graded letters, providing constructive criticisms and discussing common mistakes as necessary. Point out to the students the pros and cons of sending letters to various people on the handout. At the end of the hour read a second "situation" to the class. Students again choose "people" from their handouts and write letters to them as homework assignments.

HOUR 3: Students bring their letters to class and read them in small groups. A discussion of each letter follows the reading; students evaluate one another's work and talk about various aspects of each letter that could be improved. At the end of the hour the letters are handed in. Give students the homework assignment to invent new "situations" and write them out in paragraph form (one-half page or so in length). Each student will then write a letter to a person on the handout, based, this time, on the situation he or she has created. Students may also invent new "people" to write the letters to if you wish to expand the project in this way.

HOUR 4: Return graded letters from Hour 3 and read several well-written examples to the class. Students then read their homework assignment for this hour in small groups. Limit the discussion during this hour to the situations that have been created and the appropriateness of the letters that were written. Reserve technical criticisms for your grading of the written situations and accompanying letters, which are handed in at the end of the hour.

Toward the end of the hour, conduct a brief discussion with the students on the value of letter writing. Give specific examples to show that learning to write letters is a worthwhile endeavor, and that there might be a payoff in the future for acquiring letter writing skills now. Letters may be used for:

Personal correspondence	Sending examples of work
Introductions in business	Informing someone of something you are doing
Delivering résumés	
Requesting information	Inspiring or encouraging someone to do something
Stating opinions or intentions	
Inquiring about jobs	Asking for help

General Notes About This Project:

• This project is designed to require students to *write letters*. They should have already been introduced to the parts of a letter, letter styles, formal and informal writing methods, and what constitutes a "good" letter for a variety of situations.

• There is no right or wrong choice of person to write letters to for each situation; if a student can justify directing his or her letter to a certain person then the selection is correct. Emphasis should be placed on *justifying* a choice rather than finding the right person from a list on a handout. Any one of the people on the handout may be right for any of the situations. Evaluations should emphasize the *thinking process* that leads to a selection.

• You may want to provide envelopes for students to address, as further practice on letterwriting mechanics. These letters are *not* to be mailed.

WRITING LETTERS
Student Assignment Sheet

```
┌─────────────────────────────────────────────────────┐
│  YOUR RETURN                              ┌───────┐  │
│  ADDRESS                                  │ STAMP │  │
│                                           └───────┘  │
│                                                      │
│                                                      │
│         DR. SUSAN WEATHERSPOON                       │
│         752 WEST MAPLE STREET                        │
│         MCCLEAN, VIRGINIA  22101                     │
│                                                      │
│                                                      │
└─────────────────────────────────────────────────────┘
```

The ability to write letters is an important skill for anyone who intends to be a professional, go into business, correspond with friends, go to college, or express opinions to others. Letters are a means of making thoughts become permanent, and of telling others what is on your mind. They are a way of communicating with people almost anywhere in the world. You will find that a well-written letter is a key that unlocks many doors; it is a valuable tool for making connections and learning on your own.

Below you will find a list of fictitious people (in other words, people who do not really exist) who are all involved in one way or another with animals. Your teacher will describe a special situation and then ask you to write a letter to one of these people. Decide which "person" would be the best one to send your letter to. There is no "right" or "wrong" answer for this choice. You should, however, be able to explain *why* you think the person that you selected from this list is the best choice. Letters will be graded for proper construction, writing skills, and neatness.

1. Anna Green
   1537 Wabash Avenue
   YOUR HOMETOWN AND ZIP CODE

   Mrs. Green is the president of the local humane society. She has been concerned about the welfare of animals all her life and she uses her position to draw attention to animal cruelty. She gives speeches all over the country and writes a weekly column for the local newspaper.

2. Dr. Jonathan Potter
   3542 Wilson Drive
   New York, New York 10016

   Dr. Potter is a leading expert on reptiles and has led several expeditions for *National Geographic*. He believes in building zoos to educate the public about animals, and he calls himself an "educator who is interested in animals."

3. Dr. Susan Weatherspoon
   752 West Maple Street
   McLean, Virginia 22101

   Dr. Weatherspoon is the president of "Save the Animals," a national organization that funds efforts to prevent the needless deaths of such animals as harp seal pups (for their white fur) and dolphins (in tuna nets). She organizes regional conferences where the problems of human destruction of animal life are discussed.

4. Jack Oldfield
   1315 North Fifth Street
   Minneapolis, Minnesota 55415

   Mr. Oldfield is the editor of *Animal Sense,* a bimonthly magazine for pet owners. He emphasizes new animal care products and services. His magazine can be found in veterinarian offices and the homes of pet owners.

5. Janet Dillon
   9871 Montgomery Street
   Chicago, Illinois 60606

   Miss Dillon is the founder of "Animal Alert!" This is a group of concerned citizens who keep close track of threatened species of animals worldwide. She publishes a newsletter twice a year in which she informs the public about poor government policies, animals that are dwindling in numbers, organizations that are doing a good job of protecting animals, and predictions of future problems.

CREATIVE WRITING

Teacher Preview

Length of Project: 7 hours

Level of Independence: Basic

Goals:

1. To encourage creative use of the English language.
2. To allow students to write in a nonformal, nontechnical manner.
3. To emphasize basic skills.

During This Project Students Will:

1. Write descriptions of objects, settings, and characters.
2. Compose creative stories.
3. Demonstrate the use of proper English grammar, and correct spelling, punctuation, and capitalization in written material.
4. Present their stories to others.

Skills:

Grammar	Selecting topics
Handwriting	Concentration
Neatness	Personal motivation
Paragraphs	Sense of "quality"
Sentences	Creative expression
Spelling	Public speaking
Organizing	Self-confidence
Outlining	Writing

Handouts Provided:

- "Student Assignment Sheet"
- " 'Getting Small' Stories"

PROJECT CALENDAR:

HOUR 1: _____	HOUR 2: _____	HOUR 3: _____
Discussion of descriptive writing, with emphasis on adjectives, adverbs, similes, and metaphors. (Parts I-A, I-B, and I-C of the handout are completed.)	Students write descriptive sentences about objects that are displayed for them to observe. Sentences are read and discussed in class. (Part I-D is completed.)	During the first half of the hour, students go outside and write descriptions of an object such as a tree, a building, or a statue that has been assigned. Descriptions are read inside during the last part of the hour. (Part I-E is completed.)
HANDOUT PROVIDED		NEED SPECIAL MATERIALS STUDENTS TURN IN WORK
HOUR 4: _____	**HOUR 5:** _____	**HOUR 6:** _____
Students write descriptions of places (settings) that are pictured on posters and read their descriptions in small groups or to the class. (Part II is completed.)	Students write descriptions of a person (character) and read their descriptions in small groups or to the class. (Part III is completed.)	Written material from previous hours is returned. Students spend the rest of the hour outside studying miniature environments. The assignment for a short story is made, due next hour.
NEED SPECIAL MATERIALS STUDENTS TURN IN WORK	PREPARATION REQUIRED STUDENTS TURN IN WORK	HANDOUT PROVIDED RETURN STUDENT WORK
HOUR 7: _____	**HOUR 8:** _____	**HOUR 9:** _____
"Getting Small" stories are read in small groups or to the class and are handed in at the end of the hour.		
STUDENTS TURN IN WORK		

Lesson Plans and Notes

HOUR 1: Distribute the "Creative Writing" student assignment sheet, which will be used for the next five hours of class. Review the following four descriptive writing tools and have students record definitions for them on their assignment sheets (part I-A):

Adjectives	Similes
Adverbs	Metaphors

Students complete parts I-B and I-C of the assignment sheet during the remainder of the hour. Student definitions and sentences may be discussed in class or collected at your discretion.

Notes:

- "Creative Writing" can be introduced by reading excerpts from the work of professional writers. See the "Quotes" handout from project W-2 for some examples, or use some samples of your own choosing from the writings of authors with whom you are familiar.
- It is assumed that students have already studied adjectives, adverbs, nouns, and verbs, and are familiar with the terms "simile" and "metaphor." They need not be proficient in the use of similes or metaphors, but it is helpful if these have at least been discussed. You may want to add an hour or two in which to cover the *basics* of descriptive writing before beginning this project.

HOUR 2: Display several objects, one at a time, in the front of the room. On their assignment sheets (Part I-D) students are to write two descriptive sentences for each object, and identify adjectives, adverbs, similes, and metaphors within their writing. After showing the first object for a few minutes, call upon students to read their descriptive sentences. These sentences are discussed and critically analyzed, and the students then create a composite sentence from the best parts of the ones recited. This sentence is written on the board and recorded by students on their assignment sheets as a good example of descriptive writing. Then display the next object and repeat the writing activity. Below is a list of possible objects to use in this activity:

Model car or airplane	A globe
Apple or other fruit	Piece of crystal or cut glass
Flower	Plant and macramé hanger
Kitchen appliance	Statues, sculptures, or artwork
Aquarium	Football helmet
Broom	Doll
Golf club	Stuffed animal

HOUR 3: Students go outside with paper, pencils, and lapboards and sit around an object such as a tree, building, or statue, that has been assigned to them (Part I-E of the assignment sheet). They have 25 minutes to write one or two descriptive paragraphs about the object they are observing. Upon returning to the classroom, students spend the last 20 minutes reading their descriptions in small groups. Paragraphs are handed in at the end of the hour.

HOUR 4: Students do Part II of the assignment sheet. The hour begins with four or five large posters of settings being placed before the class (such as a sunset over the desert, a city street, a volcano erupting, a steel mill, ice floes in an artic bay, and the like). Each student's instructions are:

> "Choose one of the pictures and pretend that it is a scene from a story you are writing. Write for 20 to 30 minutes to describe the scene as graphically as possible. The plot is not important and neither are the characters. The scene can be described from the point of view of a character in the story, or by you as an outside observer. You can be a character in the story too, if you want, but your writing must in some way describe the scene. Be sure to write about colors, shapes, smells, sounds, feelings and small details as well as a general description of the setting. Don't just list the objects in the picture; be *descriptive!*"

After 25 minutes all writing stops and students read their setting descriptions, either in small groups or to the class. This is good practice for future presentations. Descriptions are handed in at the end of the hour.

HOUR 5: Students do Part III of the assignment sheet. Begin the hour by selecting a "model." Be sure it is a person who has fairly good writing skills. (Students who do not have good skills should be writing; the model does not write.) Or, you can bring in a "guest character." The model sits on a chair, or stands, in the front of the room. This person is made up to give him or her true "character." Everyone in the class is then assigned to write for 20 to 25 minutes, describing the model as if that person were being introduced as the character of a story. The setting and plot are left up to the students, but they have little importance and should not be emphasized in this project.

After 25 minutes all writing stops and the students read their descriptions in small groups or to the class. They are turned in at the end of the hour.

HOUR 6: Return all the students' written material from the first five hours and distribute the handout, "'Getting Small' Stories." Lead students into a discussion about "environments" and what they are. Be sure to place emphasis on the relative size of environments. A whale's environment is the entire ocean while a bacterium's is a drop of ocean water. Part I of the "Getting Small" handout tells students to describe an environment that is one square yard in size. They go outside and each finds his or her own square-yard area. The assignment calls for two things:

1. A comprehensive list of *everything* that can be found in the square yard. This is hands-and-knees time!

2. A one-paragraph description of the square yard. Students should write this as if they were starting a story by describing the square yard. This particular "environment" is a very important part of a story and must be carefully described so that the story can be properly told. Creativity is encouraged.

The paragraph written during this hour is used as the first paragraph in a short story that students write as homework, to be read during Hour 7. The homework assignment (part II of the handout) tells students what to include in a short story which everyone titles, "Getting Small." Each student imagines that he or she is studying environments by examining a certain piece of ground (the square yard). Suddenly some mysterious force shrinks the student to a height of one centimeter, right in the middle of his or her square yard. This environment now becomes an entire world and the story is to tell—in exciting and creative detail—all the adventures that are involved in surviving in this new world.

HOUR 7: Students read their "Getting Small" stories orally, in a small group or to the class from the front of the room. After the stories are read they are turned in to be graded for grammar, spelling, and writing skills. Poorly written papers should be rewritten and handed back in for a second review. At the end of the hour conduct a brief discussion about the general value of creative writing skills. Point out that a person who writes well is more likely to be read and therefore has a better chance to voice opinions and express creativity than someone who has not worked to become a writer. Emphasize to the students that most good writers had to *work* at their art; that there are very few "natural" writers.

General Notes About This Project:

- This project provides an excellent opportunity to emphasize the use of dictionaries and thesauruses.

- There are several uses for written material in this project. Least time consuming (in classroom hours) is to collect written material when it is completed and grade it. If you want to emphasize presentation skills along with idea sharing and critical peer analysis, small group readings can be employed. Most time consuming is to have each student present his or her work to the entire class. Other possibilities include having small groups each choose *one* of its readings to present to the entire class, or producing a bulletin board or wall display of neatly written descriptive paragraphs and stories. The "Getting Small" stories can lead to dramatizations or puppet shows. The assignment sheets for this project call for students to read their work in small groups or to the class. If you decide not to do either of these, students should be informed.

- This project can be used to teach about environments and survival, and can easily be tied into an outdoor education class, a science class, or a health class. In using it, emphasize the basic physical needs of life as well as human social needs and environmental appreciation.

CREATIVE WRITING
Student Assignment Sheet

Of all the types of writing that people do, none is more enjoyable or more satisfying than creative writing. Creative writing is a way of describing people, places, events, and feelings so that they seem real. It is like painting pictures with words. Writers use creativity when composing stories and poems, when describing objects, characters, and settings, or when expressing opinions, attitudes, and emotions. Good writers know how to use the English language to its fullest extent: they know how to construct sentences and paragraphs, and they realize the importance of an improved vocabulary. A dictionary and a thesaurus are a creative writer's most valuable tools, because they contain the perfect descriptive words for every situation.

This project emphasizes the three major components of a creative short story: objects (or "things"), settings, and characters. These parts of a short story must be described if the reader is to get a complete mental image of a scene. Follow the directions carefully as you work on this project. Each section is designed to help build some of the creative writing skills that are important to a serious writer. Your teacher will tell you which parts of the assignment sheet to complete during each of the next several class hours.

HOW WOULD YOU DESCRIBE THIS CHARACTER?

I. OBJECT DESCRIPTIONS

A. Write a definition for each of these terms:

1. Adjective: _____

_____

2. Adverb: _____

_____

3. Simile: _____

_____

4. Metaphor: _____

_____

B. Make this sentence more descriptive by rewriting it four times. Add an adjective, adverb, simile, or metaphor to each new sentence.

"The sun set behind the clouds."

1. Add an adjective: _____

_____

2. Add an adverb: _____

_____

3. Add a simile: _____

_____

4. Add a metaphor: _____

_____

C. Rewrite the sentence, "The sun set behind the clouds," as a descriptive sentence that uses any combination of adjectives, adverbs, similes, and metaphors:

_____

_____

_____

D. Several objects will be displayed in the front of the room. After studying each one for a few moments, write two descriptive sentences about it. A class sentence will be developed by discussing the ideas of various students. Be prepared to read your sentences during this discussion. Underline all adjectives, adverbs, similes, and metaphors.

Object   **Descriptive Sentence**

1. _____   a. _____

   _____

   b. _____

   _____

   Class sentence: _____

   _____

2. _____   a. _____

   _____

   b. _____

   _____

   Class sentence: _____

   _____

3. _____   a. _____

   _____

   b. _____

   _____

   Class sentence: _____

   _____

4. _____   a. _____

   _____

   b. _____

   _____

   Class sentence: _____

   _____

5. _____ a. _____

_____

b. _____

_____

Class sentence: _____

_____

E. Go outside and observe an object assigned by your teacher. On a separate piece of paper, write one or two descriptive paragraphs about the object. Assume that the object being described is an important part of a story that you are writing; perhaps it is a clue in a mystery or something the reader should remember clearly later on in the story. When class resumes, you will read your descriptive paragraphs in small groups and then hand them in.

II. SETTING DESCRIPTIONS

Several pictures, photographs, or posters are displayed on the walls of the room. Look them over carefully and choose one that would make a good setting for a story. You will not be writing a complete story for this assignment, but you *will* describe a setting, which is often the first step in story writing. On a separate piece of paper, write a one- or two-paragraph description of the scene. Be prepared to read your description to the class or in a small group during the last part of the hour. Setting descriptions will be handed in.

III. CHARACTER DESCRIPTIONS

During this hour you will be writing a character description. A model has taken his or her place at the front of the room. Your assignment is to describe this person as the main character in a short story. Concentrate on physical appearance and how the person *seems* to feel. Explain what it is that makes the person appear to be happy, sad, depressed, angry, carefree, and so forth. Use some imagination for this. If the model does not seem to be angry, for example, but you want the character to *be* angry, use descriptive vocabulary to invent a character who has lost his or her temper. Be prepared to read your character description to the class or in a small group during the last part of the hour. Character descriptions will be handed in.

Name _____ Date _____

"GETTING SMALL" STORIES

Once some of the skills for descriptive writing are mastered, a good way of applying them is to write fiction. Short stories are an excellent way to practice and improve skills for describing things to a reader. For this project you will write a short story about getting small: really small, like one centimeter tall. Such a situation offers possibilities for interesting plot development as well as opportunities for humor, suspense, tragedy, action, and character development.

Follow this assignment outline to create a story about becoming very, very small.

I. Go outside and select an area that is approximately one square yard in size (three feet by three feet). This area will be the *setting* for your story, so choose it carefully.

   A. Make a complete list of *everything* in the square yard. Examine the area carefully on your hands and knees and list the things you find. These things will become major objects in the world your story describes.

   B. Write a one-paragraph description of the square yard, from the perspective of a student who has been assigned to study a small piece of ground. For example, you might write, "One day my teacher decided to teach us about environments. I was assigned to make a close-up investigation of a small piece of ground. As I left the building I was mysteriously drawn toward an area of the school grounds that I had never visited, and for some reason I became deeply absorbed in one particular piece of ground. This tiny territory, no more than one square yard in size, was fascinating..."

II. Write a "Getting Small" story.

   A. Use the square-yard description you wrote for part I-B of this handout as an introduction to the story. Then imagine that you somehow shrink in size and now see this same environment from the perspective of a person one centimeter tall.

   B. Include these things in the story:

      1. A brief description of how you became small.

      2. At least one other character besides yourself. (This can be an insect or other animal, an imaginary being that humans know nothing about, or another person.)

      3. An explanation of how you survived in this new environment. How did you:

         a. Stay warm   d. Travel
         b. Find food and water   e. Clothe yourself
         c. Protect yourself   f. Provide shelter

      4. A simple plot

      5. A conclusion

      6. Give your story a title.

   C. The stories will be handed in. You may be asked to read your story in a small group or to the class.

STORY WRITING

Teacher Preview

Length of Project: 6 hours

Level of Independence: Intermediate

Goals:

1. To make use of the skills emphasized in the "Creative Writing" project: object, setting, character, and story descriptions.
2. To allow students to express their creativity by writing stories.
3. To require the proper use of basic writing skills.

During This Project Students Will:

1. Describe at least three characters for a story.
2. Describe a setting for a story.
3. Outline a plot for a story.
4. Write a short story.

Skills:

Listening	Outlining
Grammar	Selecting topics
Handwriting	Following project outlines
Neatness	Sense of "quality"
Paragraphs	Creative expression
Sentences	Public speaking
Self-confidence	Observing
Spelling	Personal motivation
Organizing	Writing

Handout Provided:

- "Student Assignment Sheet"

PROJECT CALENDAR:

HOUR 1: _____	**HOUR 2:** _____	**HOUR 3:** _____
Assignment sheets are handed out. Discussion of character descriptions fills the rest of the hour. Parts I and II of the assignment sheet are due next hour.	Character selections and sketches are handed in. The hour is spent discussing settings. Part III of the assignment sheet is due next hour.	Setting descriptions are turned in. The hour is spent discussing plot. Part IV of the assignment sheet is due next hour.
HANDOUT PROVIDED PREPARATION REQUIRED	STUDENTS TURN IN WORK PREPARATION REQUIRED	STUDENTS TURN IN WORK PREPARATION REQUIRED
HOUR 4: _____	**HOUR 5:** _____	**HOUR 6:** _____
Plot descriptions are turned in. The hour is spent discussing short stories. No written assignment.	Character descriptions, setting descriptions, and plot outlines are returned. Students begin writing short stories (Part V of the assignment sheet).	Students turn in their finished stories; discussion of the skills needed to produce a short story.
PREPARATION REQUIRED	RETURN STUDENT WORK	STUDENTS TURN IN WORK
HOUR 7: _____	**HOUR 8:** _____	**HOUR 9:** _____

Lesson Plans and Notes

HOUR 1: Give out the "Story Writing" assignment sheet and explain it, point-by-point. Spend the remainder of the hour discussing character descriptions and the reasons for character development in story writing. A few character descriptions from such classic writers as Dickens, Twain, Melville, Tolkien, Steinbeck, or any other author may be read to the class. Come to class prepared with several examples. At the end of the hour assign students to complete parts I and II of the handout, to be handed in at the beginning of the next hour.

Note:

- Students can be assigned the task of finding their own examples of character descriptions but add an hour to the project for them to bring such materials to class. It is advisable to expose students to a variety of writers and styles (and use of vocabulary!) as they prepare to write their own stories.

HOUR 2: Students hand in their homework assignment from Hour 1. Spend time this hour discussing settings and reading excerpts from various books. The assignment, due at the beginning of the next hour, is Part III of the handout.

HOUR 3: Students hand in their "setting descriptions" and move on to a discussion of plot: what it is and how it is used in various well-known stories. The plots in movies and television shows that students have seen can also be discussed. The main point is that a good plot must be *planned* so that the story moves logically from beginning to conclusion and so that all of the events in the story make sense. The assignment, due at the beginning of the next hour, is Part IV of the handout.

Note:

- A good method of explaining plot is to use children's books, especially ones written for children younger than your students. Many of these stories have straightforward, simple plots that can be quickly described and analyzed. Even fairy tales such as *Cinderella* and *Little Red Riding Hood* can provide examples of plot and narrative flow.

HOUR 4: Students hand in their plot outlines. Spend the rest of the hour discussing and reading short stories from student readers and from other books that are brought in. No writing can be done during this hour because the students' character descriptions, setting descriptions, and plot outlines must be checked and returned before story writing begins.

HOUR 5: Return the character descriptions, setting descriptions, and plot outlines to the class. Students who must rewrite any of their work spend this hour beginning that task. The other students begin working on their stories (Part V of the handout). Set a due date for submission of all *rewritten* material and a final due date for completion of the stories.

HOUR 6: Students turn in their short stories and spend the remainder of the hour discussing the value of story-writing skills and how they can be used by students in the future. Aside from the simple pleasure of writing original material, there are other benefits from creative writing which are very important. Primary among these is self-confidence: confidence in one's own ability to express oneself. This confidence flows into all areas of communication and helps establish a sense of individuality in students. Other benefits include an improved vocabulary, an enjoyable way to practice basic English grammar skills, an opportunity to express deep feelings, beliefs, and attitudes in story form, and a chance to work on skills that apply to such occupations as journalist, advertiser, or writer.

Note:

- Students may be asked to read their stories to the class, but this is time consuming. If you use oral reading, consider doing it in small groups. Or, after collecting and reading the stories, choose two or three to read to the class before they are returned to the students.

General Note About This Project:

- This project can be used for independent learning if students are prepared to work on their own to complete the requirements outlined on the assignment sheet. You can give it to a few students as a special project or to the entire class as an "independent assignment." The only time requirement is the few minutes needed to hand out assignment sheets, explain the project, and set a due date on which to collect completed work. If the project is conducted this way, the level of independence becomes advanced.

Name _____ Date _____

STORY WRITING
Student Assignment Sheet

Writing a short story is a true form of self-expression. When you take pen in hand and sit down before a blank piece of paper, it is your mind power that generates a story: characters, settings, plot, conclusion. There are many reasons for writing a short story. Some people write just for fun: to weave exciting or interesting tales. Others use fiction as a way of explaining or teaching something about the real world: they write short stories as lessons about certain issues or topics. There are authors who use short stories to record experiences from their own lives, and others who write as a way of demonstrating their feelings. A short story is a vehicle that delivers a message. As the author, you decide what the message is.

Follow this outline as you write. Read it carefully and do each part in order.

I. Character Selection (at least three)

Decide what kinds of characters you want to use to tell your story. They can be people, animals, plants, rocks, or anything else as long as they have personalities and names. Identify the characters below (you are required to create three characters, but you can have more if you wish). Tell what kind of a "being" each character is (such as woman, boy, wolf, oak tree, ant, chunk of coal) and give it/him/her a name:

Kind of Being   *Name*

1. _____

2. _____

3. _____

4. _____

5. _____

II. Character Sketches (at least three)

Describe at least three characters in your story. Write a one- or two-paragraph character sketch for each one. Describe as many of the following things as possible:

A. What does the character look like?
B. Is the character evil/good, happy/sad, brave/cowardly, pretty/ugly, selfish/charitable, rich/poor, smart/stupid, and so forth?
C. What do other characters think about this character?
D. Where does the character live?
E. What is the character's history? Has anything exciting or important happened in his or her life?
F. How does the character fit into the story?
G. Is there anything else that should be explained or described about the character?

III. Setting

The story should take place in a specific setting that can be visualized in your mind and described in words. Write a one- or two-paragraph description of your story's setting. Include the following things:

A. Explain where the setting is in general: a forest, a city, a mountain, a train, an anthill, and so forth.

B. Describe the surroundings in some detail (objects such as trees or buildings, colors, smells, sounds).

C. Describe anything about the setting that is important to the story (the extreme cold of a winter morning or the dryness of a drought-stricken forest, for example).

D. Explain how the characters fit into the setting or, if they *don't* fit, explain how they came to be there. More than one setting can be used, but you are required to write a description for each one, so don't get carried away.

IV. Plot

The plot is what holds a story together. All writing should begin with a plan; the goal is to produce a carefully constructed story that is easy to follow and understand. An outline is a good way to plan a story and develop a plot.

First, make a *list* of all the main characters, descriptions, and actions that are to be included in the story. Next, put these things into an *outline* that shows the order in which they will appear; then develop a way to begin and end your story. Finally, add detail to each part of the outline so that when you start to actually write the story there is a solid base of ideas to fuel your creative mind.

In review, the outline should reveal these things:

A. How the story begins.

B. When each character is introduced.

C. At which points you will describe scenes for the reader to visualize.

D. At which points there will be action in the story.

E. Other information a reader may need to understand such as clues, time frames, cultural traditions, relationships, and the like.

F. How the story ends.

V. Story

Write a story which follows the outline you have developed. Minimum length is four pages. You will be given due dates for handing in your preliminary character descriptions, setting descriptions, and plot outline. After these are checked and returned, you will begin writing the story. A due date for the finished story will then be set. You may be asked to read your story to the class or it may be read by the teacher after it is graded. The story will be graded for:

A. Originality and creativity.

B. Your ability to produce and follow an outline.

C. Grammar, spelling, sentence structure, and other basic writing skills.

D. Effort and self-discipline.

VI. Think of a title for your story

VII. Due Dates

A. Character selections and sketches_____

B. Setting description(s)_____

C. Plot outline_____

D. Rewritten material_____

E. Finished story_____

ROOTS:
A FAMILY HISTORY PROJECT

Teacher Preview

General Explanation:

"Roots" is a writing project that focuses on the life of each individual student. Students write papers about their teacher, their family, themselves, and the world in which they are growing up. These papers, after being graded, are sealed in time capsules made by the students. (The project can be shortened by five hours if the time capsules are not made in class. There is a "Roots Time-Line" at the end of the lesson plan material to help you schedule this project.) Because considerable time is needed for students to work on the assignments, and for you to grade the written material, the 14 classroom hours for "Roots" are spread over a nine-week period.

Length of Project: 14 hours

Level of Independence: Intermediate

Goals:

1. To provide motivation to write by emphasizing family heritage.
2. To involve parents and other family members in the student's education.
3. To require the proper use of basic writing skills as students write about themselves, their families, and some important events of the world they live in.
4. To place emphasis on independent learning.

During This Project Students Will:

1. Take accurate notes while conducting interviews.
2. Assemble information for parent biographies.
3. Write essays from prepared outlines.
4. Organize outlines for autobiographies.
5. Design and produce time capsules.

Skills:

Collecting data	Spelling
Interviewing	Organizing
Listening	Outlining

Summarizing	Selecting topics
Grammar	Following project outlines
Handwriting	Meeting deadlines
Neatness	Sense of "quality"
Paragraphs	Creative expression
Personal motivation	Self-confidence
Sentences	Accepting responsibility
Writing	

Handouts Provided:

- "Student Assignment Sheet"
- Student Research Guide (see Appendix) "Outlining"

PROJECT CALENDAR:

HOUR 1: _____ Discussion of family heritage and introduction to the project. Students are given an assignment sheet. HANDOUT PROVIDED	**HOUR 2:** _____ Teacher interview: students ask questions and take notes on answers. A due date for papers is set. *These are collected and graded before Hour 3.*	**HOUR 3:** _____ Teacher interview papers are returned and discussed. Students prepare for a parent interview by suggesting interview questions. Due date for parent biographies is posted. RETURN STUDENT WORK
HOUR 4: _____ Students turn in finished parent biographies. The hour is spent discussing the interviews. STUDENTS TURN IN WORK	**HOUR 5:** _____ An example of how to outline an autobiography is put on the board. A due date for autobiography outlines is posted, along with a due date for finished autobiographies. *Outlines are handed in, graded, and returned before autobiographies are written: this work is done before Hour 6.* HANDOUT PROVIDED	**HOUR 6:** _____ Students turn in autobiographies, and parent biographies are returned. The hour is a quiet period for rewriting parent interviews. STUDENTS TURN IN WORK RETURN STUDENT WORK
HOUR 7: _____ One major current event is outlined on the board while it is explained verbally. Students record the outline as notes. Students are encouraged to expand their outlines before Hour 8. PREPARATION REQUIRED	**HOUR 8:** _____ Autobiographies are returned. Students write for the hour about the current event topic outlined during Hour 7. They may use their outlines. Papers are handed in. STUDENTS TURN IN WORK RETURN STUDENT WORK	**HOUR 9:** _____ Current events papers are returned. Students go through newspapers and magazines to find material for their time capsules. NEED SPECIAL MATERIALS RETURN STUDENT WORK

PROJECT CALENDAR (continued):

HOUR 10: _____	HOUR 11: _____	HOUR 12: _____
Return all rewritten material. Time capsules are filled with family history and current events materials. Cover capsules with papier-mâché.	Dry time capsules are painted.	Painted capsules are varnished.
RETURN STUDENT WORK NEED SPECIAL MATERIALS	NEED SPECIAL MATERIALS	NEED SPECIAL MATERIALS
HOUR 13: _____	HOUR 14: _____	HOUR 15: _____
Capsules are varnished a second time.	Discussion of the value of studying one's roots and handing the history of one generation on to the next; capsules are taken home.	
NEED SPECIAL MATERIALS		
HOUR 16: _____	HOUR 17: _____	HOUR 18: _____

Lesson Plans and Notes

HOUR 1: Draw students into a discussion of family heritage by having them tell stories of family adventures, experiences, or history. The TV mini-series, "Roots," can be discussed, but the main focus is on the value and self-satisfaction of knowing your own history and getting to know your parents and grandparents better. Give out the "Roots" assignment sheet and discuss each assignment, placing special emphasis on the meaningfulness of this project to older people: it gives them a sense of passing their wisdom and knowledge on to the next generation. This discussion serves the purpose of exciting the students, "firing them up" for the work involved in interviewing, outlining, notetaking, and writing, writing, writing. Point out to the students that everything that is written for this course is graded for handwriting, spelling, grammar, punctuation, capitalization, sentence structure, and paragraph formation.

Notes:

- Pay particular attention to the final five hours of the course, which is essentially an art project. The time capsule is meant to transport all the "Roots" information that has been gathered and recorded on to the *next* generation (the students' own children, 25 years from now). Therefore, suggest to the students that, above all else, they should want to show their *very best writing* to their own children. This is an excellent form of self-motivation.

- Be aware that some of your students probably come from single-parent families, and some may be adopted. Special situations may arise that you should be sensitive to.

- It is a good idea to determine the due dates for all "Roots" assignments before the project begins. During the first hour students can be given the dates to record in the spaces provided on the assignment sheet. To figure out what these dates will be, sit down with the "Roots Time-Line" (provided at the end of the lesson plans) and a calendar. In the boxes provided, pencil in each assignment's due date. *Notice that some work is handed in and returned between class hours.*

HOUR 2: Have students interview you by raising their hands and being called on one at a time to ask a question. Students should take notes on your answers as everyone is responsible for all the information given. This is sometimes a slow, tedious process of repetition, but it is necessary in order for most students to learn how to listen and write. At the end of the hour, after the interview, remind students of what day the teacher interview papers are due, and write this date in a permanent place on the board. Have students write it on their assignment sheets as well. The papers are graded for writing, accuracy, and completeness. *Teacher interview papers are collected and graded before Hour 3.*

Notes:

- The "Roots" project involves a *lot* of grading, which takes time. Be sure to schedule assignments so that you can get things graded in time to start the next activity. If you start activities one right after the other an immense backlog of grading can accumulate, and the job will seem almost overwhelming. Spread the course out so this doesn't happen. Before the project begins, determine how much time you want between the hours of instruction. A time-line is provided at the end of the lesson plans which gives suggested intervals.

- The teacher interview requires students to ask questions about your life history. They take notes and write short biographies about *you*. This gives them practice at interviewing, and their papers can be graded more easily because the questions and answers are known: it will be obvious which students took good notes, and whether any information was "concocted." Be prepared for some strange and possibly embarrassing questions, and let students know what the limits or parameters for their questions are.

HOUR 3: Spend this hour preparing for the parent interview. First, return the teacher interview papers, and point out common mistakes. Papers that must be rewritten are assigned as homework, with a set due date. Then, through class discussion, have students generate a list of questions that could be asked of parents. Students are responsible for getting these questions into their notes. (It helps to write the questions on the board.) At the end of the hour students are equipped with a list of questions they can use for their parent interviews. After holding the parent interviews, students are to write the biographies. Many students are motivated to go far beyond the minimum assignment, and they should be encouraged to do so. Announce the due date for these biographies; record it on the board and on the student handout.

HOUR 4: Students turn in their finished biographies and family histories. Finish the hour by discussing interesting facts and stories that have been gathered in the process of doing this project.

Note:

- One of the greatest lessons learned from this assignment is how to get an assignment done that is due "two weeks from now." There will be students who don't do the assignment, and others who do a shoddy job. Be prepared with make-up assignments or some other kind of work to show that it is not wise to ignore such an important project. Also, when the parent biographies are handed back, poorly written ones should be rewritten as a homework assignment. Or you may choose to have students rewrite them in class, in which case something special should be available for those who do not have to rewrite. Be strict in the requirements for rewritten work; it is very important for students to see the value in writing well the *first* time something is handed in. Also, when grading, consider each student's basic ability and do not demand the impossible from students who are seriously trying to improve their writing. Reward effort as well as quality.

HOUR 5: Distribute the "Outlining" handout from the Student Research Guide (see Appendix). Following instructions on the handout, outline a fictional autobiography on the board, using information from different students for the various topics and subtopics. Be sure to point out that the outline can be greatly expanded; illustrate this on the board by expanding the fictional autobiography.

At the end of this hour, instruct students to outline their own lives, and encourage them to gather information by talking to parents and other relatives. Set a due date (three or four days after Hour 5) for submission of the outlines to you to be graded and returned. Students then have one week from the day they receive their graded outlines to write their autobiographies and turn them in at the beginning of Hour 6. Outlines that must be rewritten are an *overnight homework assignment*.

In summary, between Hours 5 and 6:

1. Students write autobiography outlines.
2. Outlines are turned in on the due date.
3. You grade the outlines and return them.
4. Students write their autobiographies, which are due Hour 6.

See the "Roots Time Line" for help in scheduling these assignments and due dates.

Note:

• To be sure that poor work is being rewritten, you might designate a study hall period or quiet reading time when people who have "Roots" make-up work must do it. This allows you to help those students who really need it. Hour 6 would be good for this purpose.

HOUR 6: Students turn in their autobiographies. Parent biographies are returned. Devote the rest of the hour to quiet time: those who have to rewrite their parent biographies work on them, and the rest may read or work on their projects.

HOUR 7: Spend this hour outlining a major current event on the board. Have this outline already prepared and in proper order before the hour begins. Student input may change it somewhat, but its basic form should be well in hand before the class begins. The topics will change year-to-year because they should be timely. For example, a presidential election or the Olympics is a good topic when it is happening, but would hardly be an appropriate topic one or two years after it occurred. As the outline is constructed on the board, present additional information in the form of a story or lecture. The event being outlined really is a story, and by outlining it you are helping students remember it. Take time to explain *why* something happened, even though the outline records only that it *did* happen. At the end of this hour students have a fairly extensive outline of at least one current event. One week from this day they will bring their outlines to class and write essays from them. (Students are allowed to use their outlines while they write.) These essays are to be written in sentences and paragraphs. The interim week is for students to improve and embellish their outlines, ask questions, watch the news, find more facts, and practice writing from their outlines.

Notes:

- This activity is designed to be conducted concurrently with a current events course that focuses on the topic being outlined and written about. If you have no such course, add one or two hours before the outlining activity, and simply discuss related topics with your class to familiarize the students with them. Assign the students to watch the evening news for a week to open their eyes to what is happening.

- Decide upon the topic for the "Current Events" paper well before the project begins. Watch the news, read magazines and newspapers, brush up on a little history, and carefully prepare an outline that is informative, interesting, inclusive, and accurate. It is important to thoroughly explain this information to students so that the outline becomes a story. This project teaches students how to prepare for and take an *essay test.*

HOUR 8: One week after Hour 7, return the graded autobiographies. Have students write from their outlines for the remainder of the hour. At the end of the hour, they hand in their essays and their outlines, to be graded for writing skills, accuracy, and proficiency in following an outline. Return these graded essays in Hour 9, again instructing that poorly written papers be rewritten. Tell the students that in the next hour they will collect materials for their time capsules. Those who can are encouraged to bring in newspapers, magazines, and catalogs for Hour 9.

HOUR 9: Current events papers are returned. Students spend the hour going through newspapers, magazines, and other materials they have brought in, looking for items to put in their time capsules (pictures of fashions, cars, people, advertising, prices, editorials, headlines, current events, and so forth).

Note:

- Materials for filling time capsules (along with finished papers) should be available. Students are asked to bring things in, but you should also supply as much as possible. Catalogs, fashion magazines, car magazines, sports magazines, and many other publications are good sources of the kinds of things today's students would like to show tomorrow's kids.

HOUR 10: Return all rewritten papers. Students fill their time capsules with their "Roots" papers and other materials. These capsules are one-gallon, wide-mouth plastic containers obtained from school cafeterias and restaurants around town. When the lids are tightly screwed on, the capsules are securely sealed with papier-mâché. Wheat paste (or flour), strips of newspaper, and water are necessary for this. The wheat paste should be mixed fairly thin, and at *least* two layers of papier-mâché should be applied to each capsule. Three is better. The capsules are placed on waxed paper; they should be turned over occasionally so that every part dries thoroughly. This takes at least two to three days.

HOUR 11: Have students paint the dry papier-mâchéd time capsules with poster paints. Students should be allowed to paint their capsules any way they want. Poster paint dries quickly, but the capsules should again be placed on waxed paper, at least overnight.

> SAFETY PRECAUTION: The following two hours involve varnishing. The area where varnishing occurs must be well ventilated. Have paint thinner in jars around the room and plenty of rags for wiping hands and cleaning up. These materials are poisonous and flammable, so caution must be exercised when using them. It is a good idea to have additional adult supervision at this time, such as parent volunteers or school aides. If adequate facilities for varnishing cannot be furnished, the project should end after the capsules have been painted.

HOUR 12: Have students coat the top nine-tenths of the painted capsules with varnish. Do not varnish the bottoms because there must be a dry area to rest them on while the varnish dries. Instead of varnish, you may want to use a polyurethane spray but use it outside. This makes the job easier although more expensive.

HOUR 13: Turn the capsules upside down and varnish the bottoms. The rest of the capsules can be given a second coat also (except for the tops, on which the capsules are resting).

> *Note:*
>
> - A second, and even a third, coat of varnish is not a bad idea, but it is time consuming. You may want to suggest that students give their time capsules more coats of varnish at home (under parent supervision). Also, be aware of how messy varnish can be! Be prepared with paint thinner, rags, and lots of newspaper. Plan all of your time capsule activities for the end of the day, if possible, so that wet capsules can remain on desk tops over night. When the varnish is dry, students can take their capsules home. Tell them to let *their* children open them when *they* are 11 (or 12 or whatever), so they can add new material and make new time capsules for the next generation. Kids seem to really like this idea of preserving something of themselves for the future.

HOUR 14: Spend the hour talking about the value of communicating with future generations. This is an excellent way to initiate a discussion about how things change. Will the items that were included in the time capsules seem odd or old-fashioned to children 20 or 30 years from now? Will it be interesting for today's students to see the contents of their own time capsules when they are adults? The discussion includes a brief description of the kinds of things some students included in their capsules. Students take their finished capsules home.

General Notes About This Project:

- This project is an excellent way to bring parents into their children's education in an active way. Don't overlook this valuable opportunity to make use of parents. Some groundwork for this project can be laid by talking with parents prior to the start of the project. You may want to begin "Roots" right after the fall, or first-term, parent conferences.

- Outlining is required for the Autobiography and Current Events papers. It is a good idea to introduce students to outlining before the "Roots" project is begun. Or, add an hour to the project schedule and use "Roots" to *teach* outlining.

- This project offers opportunities to focus on a number of basic writing and language arts skills: notetaking, outlining, writing first person narrative, writing third person narrative, writing essays. Also, the importance of producing rough drafts and following outlines can be stressed. Obviously, emphasis can be placed on grammar, spelling, sentence structure, and paragraph development, to whatever extent is desired. You may want to use the "Writing Evaluation" sheet provided in the Appendix.

ROOTS TIME LINE

This time line is provided to illustrate how the project should be scheduled, to allow enough time for students to complete their assignments, and to ensure that everything can be graded within the time frame. The schedule shown here requires nine weeks, which represents one quarter of a school year, so "Roots" can be used as a first, second, third, or fourth quarter project. Since the final week involves making time capsules, grades can be compiled before the project is actually finished. The chart following the time line lists each activity and shows when it is assigned, collected, and returned. It also indicates how much time is available for grading.

ROOTS TIME LINE

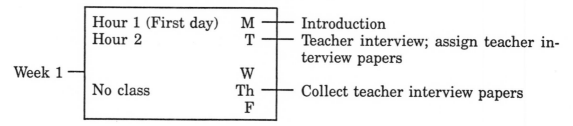

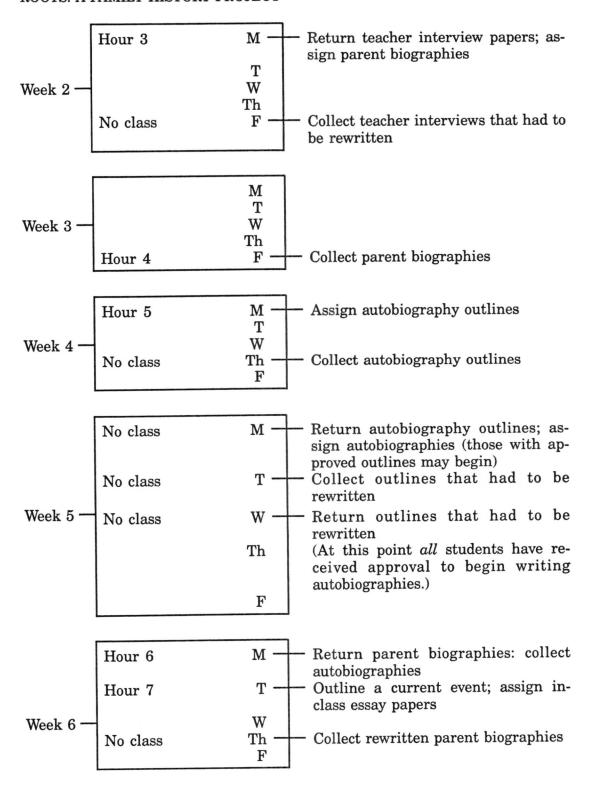

Week 2

Hour 3	M	— Return teacher interview papers; assign parent biographies
	T	
	W	
	Th	
No class	F	— Collect teacher interviews that had to be rewritten

Week 3

	M	
	T	
	W	
	Th	
Hour 4	F	— Collect parent biographies

Week 4

Hour 5	M	— Assign autobiography outlines
	T	
	W	
No class	Th	— Collect autobiography outlines
	F	

Week 5

No class	M	— Return autobiography outlines; assign autobiographies (those with approved outlines may begin)
No class	T	— Collect outlines that had to be rewritten
No class	W	— Return outlines that had to be rewritten
	Th	(At this point *all* students have received approval to begin writing autobiographies.)
	F	

Week 6

Hour 6	M	— Return parent biographies: collect autobiographies
Hour 7	T	— Outline a current event; assign in-class essay papers
	W	
No class	Th	— Collect rewritten parent biographies
	F	

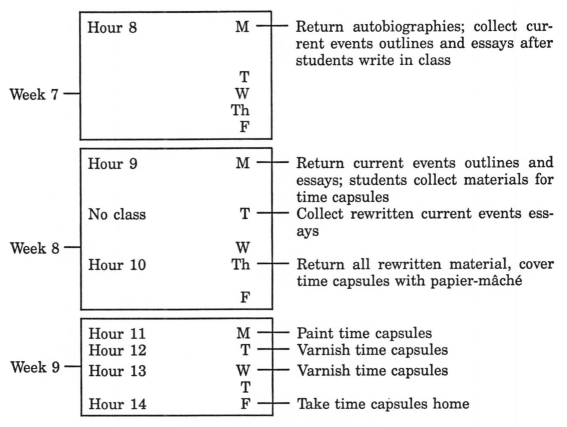

Week 7 — Hour 8   M — Return autobiographies; collect current events outlines and essays after students write in class
T
W
Th
F

Week 8 —
Hour 9   M — Return current events outlines and essays; students collect materials for time capsules
No class   T — Collect rewritten current events essays
W
Hour 10   Th — Return all rewritten material, cover time capsules with papier-mâché
F

Week 9 —
Hour 11   M — Paint time capsules
Hour 12   T — Varnish time capsules
Hour 13   W — Varnish time capsules
T
Hour 14   F — Take time capsules home

ROOTS ACTIVITY CHART

Activity	Assigned	Collected	Returned	Grading Time*
1. Teacher Interview	Week 1 Tue.	Week 1 Thur.	Week 2 Mon.	4 days
2. Parent Biographies	Week 2 Mon.	Week 3 Fri.	Week 6 Mon.	17 days
3. Autobiography Outlines	Week 4 Mon.	Week 4 Thur.	Week 5 Mon.	4 days
4. Autobiographies	Week 5 Mon.	Week 6 Mon.	Week 7 Mon.	7 days
5. Current Events Essays	Week 6 Tue.	Week 7 Mon.	Week 8 Mon.	7 days
6. Rewritten Papers	As Needed	As time line Indicates	Week 8 Thur.	Varies

*Grading time includes weekend days

Name _____ Date _____

ROOTS
Student Assignment Sheet

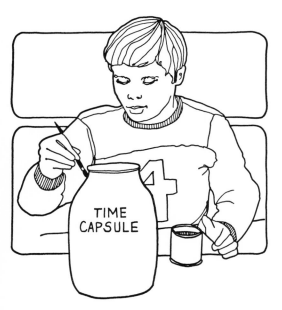

The "Roots" course provides an opportunity for your family history, your life story, and a lot of other information to be passed on to the next generation by means of a time capsule. It is exciting to think that you can pass along knowledge, experiences, and personal memorabilia that might otherwise be lost or forgotten. It is also interesting to think of opening this time capsule 25 years from now and seeing a glimpse of yourself in a former time.

During this project you will also be learning a number of skills that are basics everyone should have. Skills like writing, outlining, notetaking, self-discipline, and meeting due dates will be emphasized.

The "Roots" project consists of four separate writing assignments that will be included in your time capsule. Everything you write will be handed in and graded. There are rewriting requirements for work that is sloppy or incomplete. This handout describes each of the "Roots" assignments and the time capsule which completes the project. Keep in mind as you write each paper that it will be read a generation from now by you, your children, and your friends who will be very interested in what you, and the world, were like at your present age—so do a good job!

I. TEACHER INTERVIEW

Using a press conference format the class will interview the teacher about his or her life, particularly as a youngster. This interview teaches you how to take accurate notes while listening to answers that are given orally. Listen carefully for important dates, facts, and interesting stories. Write down key words and phrases which you can recognize later since there won't be time to write out complete sentences. At the end of class your homework assignment will be to write a paper about the teacher, using your notes from this hour.

The Teacher Interview will be on this date: _____

The Teacher Interview Paper is due on: _____

II. PARENT BIOGRAPHY

You and your classmates will develop a list of questions that can be used during parent interviews. Use these questions, along with any others you think of, to find out some of your parent's personal history. The assignment is for you to sit down with one parent and talk about what life was like when he or she was your age and, then, using the notes from this interview, write a biography about your parent. You are not limited to just one interview; grandparents, aunts, uncles, or other relatives may be able to give you even more information for your parent biography. Or you may want to write a biography about each person interviewed.

The list of questions will be developed in class on this date: _____

The Parent Biography is due on: _____
   (minimum length: 4 pages)

III. AUTOBIOGRAPHY

Your class will develop an outline for a fictional autobiography on the board during class. Outlining is a necessary step in writing papers since it organizes information and provides a "plan" for presenting each idea that you want to include in a report or paper. After your class has developed the fictional outline, your assignment will be to write an outline about *your* life. This outline will be turned in later and graded. After it is approved you will have one week to write your autobiography, using the outline as a guide.

The discussion of outlining will be on this date: _____

The outline will be handed in on this date: _____

Your autobiography (with attached outline) is due on: _____
   (minimum length: 3 pages)

IV. CURRENT EVENTS

Your class will outline and discuss a current topic—something that is a major event in the world right now. This topic will be history 25 years from now and it will be interesting *then* to see what kinds of things were happening "way back when." One week after the current events outline is made you will come to class with *your* outline about the topic and write a report. You will have most of the hour to work so use the preceding week to prepare a more detailed outline from which to write your current events paper. Keep the outline on your desk and refer to it often as you write. The reports will be handed in and graded. There is no minimum requirement; you will write for one hour and turn in what you have written. This is called an "in-class essay."

A current events outline will be made on this date: _____

The in-class essay will be written on this date: _____

V. REWRITING REPORTS

After "Roots" papers are graded they will be returned. If work is sloppy, incomplete, or if you have made writing mistakes, you will be required to rewrite it and hand it back in. It is to your advantage to do your best work the first time.

VI. TIME CAPSULE

When all of your written material has received a passing grade, you will seal it in a time capsule, along with anything else you wish to preserve for the future. Consider including such things as:

Newspaper ads	Personal notes
Magazine articles	Awards
Photographs	Drawings, poetry, stories
Coins	A family tree
Cassette tapes	Anything else you can think of

"MY GRANDPARENTS"

CLASSROOM PRODUCTIONS

Teacher Preview

General Explanation:

For this project students work in small groups, choose topics, conduct research, write scripts, and present an informative fifteen-minute final presentation (or "production") to the class. These productions take the form of puppet shows, newscasts, role plays, reenactments, or dramatic presentations.

Length of Project: 20 hours

Level of Independence: Advanced

Goals:

1. To require the use of research skills as students learn about specific topics.
2. To provide a purpose, or an application, for written reports.
3. To promote the concept of "kids teaching kids."
4. To place emphasis on independent learning.

During This Project Students Will:

1. Work with others in small groups.
2. Select appropriate topics for study.
3. Assemble information for reports.
4. Prepare proper bibliography cards.
5. Design classroom presentations.
6. Write well-organized scripts.
7. Present final productions.

Skills:

Preparing bibliographies	Identifying problems
Collecting data	Meeting deadlines
Interviewing	Working with others
Library skills	Accepting responsibility
Listening	Concentration
Making notecards	Controlling behavior
Summarizing	Individualized study habits
Grammar	Persistence

Handwriting
Neatness
Paragraphs
Sentences
Spelling
Group planning
Organizing
Setting objectives
Selecting topics
Divergent-convergent-
evaluative thinking
Following and changing plans
Following project outlines
Writing

Sharing space
Time management
Personal motivation
Sense of "quality"
Setting personal goals
Creative expression
Creating presentation strategies
Drawing and sketching
Poster making
Public speaking
Self-confidence
Teaching others
Working with limited resources
Taking care of materials

Handouts Provided:

- "Student Assignment Sheet"
- "Choosing a Topic"
- "Presentation Methods"
- "Student Evaluation Sheet"
- Teacher Introduction to the Student Research Guide (optional; see Appendix)
  a. "Writing Evaluation"
  b. "Notecard Evaluation"
  c. "Poster Evaluation"
  d. "Oral Presentation Evaluation"
- Student Research Guide (optional; see Appendix)
  a. "Notecards and Bibliographies"
  b. "Dewey Decimal Classification System"
  c. "The Card Catalog"
  d. *"Readers' Guide to Periodical Literature"*
  e. "Audio-Visual and Written Information Guides"
  f. "Where to Go or Write for Information"
  g. "Poster Display Sheet"
  h. "Things to Check Before Giving Your Presentation"
  i. "Visual Aids for the Oral Presentation"
  j. "Things to Remember When Presenting Your Project"
  k. "Daily Log"
  l. "Blank Skills Chart"

PROJECT CALENDAR:

HOUR 1: _____ Students receive three project handouts (all but the evaluation sheet) and optional handouts from the Student Research Guide. The project is explained; small groups are formed. HANDOUTS PROVIDED	**HOUR 2:** _____ Small groups choose leaders and secretaries, and decide upon topics. NEED SPECIAL MATERIALS	**HOUR 3:** _____ Introduction to scriptwriting. PREPARATION REQUIRED
HOUR 4: _____ Students plan the visual portion of a simple practice script. PREPARATION REQUIRED	**HOUR 5:** _____ Students write simple scripts about a topic supplied by the teacher. PREPARATION REQUIRED STUDENTS TURN IN WORK	**HOUR 6:** _____ Students turn in notecards, bibliographies, and written research papers; small groups begin planning their productions. STUDENTS TURN IN WORK
HOUR 7: _____ Small groups continue to plan their productions.	**HOUR 8:** _____ Research papers, notecards, and bibliographies are returned. In small groups, students begin writing production scripts and designing visual displays. RETURN STUDENT WORK	**HOUR 9:** _____ In small groups, students write scripts and work on visual displays. NEED SPECIAL MATERIALS

PROJECT CALENDAR:

HOUR 10: _____	HOUR 11: _____	HOUR 12: _____
Work on scripts and visuals.	Work on scripts and visuals.	Work on scripts and visuals.
NEED SPECIAL MATERIALS	NEED SPECIAL MATERIALS	NEED SPECIAL MATERIALS

HOUR 13: _____	HOUR 14: _____	HOUR 15: _____
Work on scripts and visuals.	Finish scripts and visuals. At the end of the hour group leaders turn in finished scripts, visual displays, and props.	Scripts and visuals are returned to group leaders; discussion of areas that need improvement. Small groups add finishing touches to their materials.
NEED SPECIAL MATERIALS	NEED SPECIAL MATERIALS STUDENTS TURN IN WORK	RETURN STUDENT WORK

HOUR 16: _____	HOUR 17: _____	HOUR 18: _____
Dress rehearsals: small groups practice their productions.	Presentations.	Presentations.

PROJECT CALENDAR:

HOUR 19: _____	HOUR 20: _____	HOUR 21: _____
Presentations.	Final discussion of the project and of skills gained. Students fill out evaluation forms. HANDOUT PROVIDED	
HOUR 22: _____	HOUR 23: _____	HOUR 24: _____
HOUR 25: _____	HOUR 26: _____	HOUR 27: _____

Lesson Plans and Notes

HOUR 1: Give students the three "Classroom Productions" handouts (all but the evaluation sheet), and carefully explain the entire project. Assign students to small groups (4 to 6 students); the best method is to assign them to groups according to their compatibility. Tell each group that during the next hour it will decide upon a presentation topic and each member of the group will identify a specific topic to study individually for a written research report. Optional handouts from the Student Research Guide should also be given out and discussed this hour.

HOUR 2: Each small group meets to choose a leader and a secretary, and to decide upon a group topic and a specific topic for each group member. At the end of the hour group leaders turn in a list of their research topics.

Tell students that they may begin working on their individual research projects right away and set a date when these papers are due (Hour 6). Have students record this date on assignment sheets. The next three class hours (3, 4, and 5) will be used to learn scriptwriting.

Notes:

- Students will hand in their research papers, complete with notecards and bibliographies, at the beginning of the sixth hour, so the project schedule should be planned accordingly. It takes most students approximately two weeks to produce an informative research report. Some students can complete the assignment in one week, but that should be the minimum time allowed.

- Be sure to evaluate the topic choices that students make. Don't let anyone pursue a topic that has insufficient information available or that is frivolous in nature.

- The assignment sheet tells students that each group secretary will be given a special notebook and a file drawer in which to store materials. These things should be provided during the second hour, after secretaries have been selected.

HOUR 3: Introduce students to scriptwriting in a simple, straightforward manner: they are to write their productions so that the spoken (audio) portion is on one side of a divided page and the accompanying visual portion is described on the other side. For example:

SCRIPT SAMPLE

Visual	Audio
Poster: map of the Middle East	BRIAN: Lebanon is located in the Middle East on the Mediterranean Sea, just north of Israel. Syria is Lebanon's neighbor to the east and north. Syria has played a big role in Lebanon's recent history.
Collage: pictures and drawings of soldiers	SUSAN: Many soldiers from many nations have marched through the land of Lebanon over the ages. Syria sent its soldiers into Lebanon in the mid 1970s to stop a civil war, and they have stayed ever since. The leaders of Syria think Lebanon should be a part of "greater Syria." Warfare in Lebanon has brought in soldiers from France, Italy, Israel, and the U.S., to name a few.
Poster: photographs from news magazines	BRIAN: Today Lebanon is a country torn apart....etc.

A script example should be provided for students to examine and discuss. Point out that a script allows for creative staging and interpretation. There are many plans and decisions for each group to make beyond what is actually written in the script. Where will the posters or other visuals be located? How will things be pointed out during the presentation? How big should the visuals be? This hour's discussion should leave students feeling that they understand the *purpose* of a script and its organizational structure.

HOUR 4: Students plan the *visual* portion of a simple practice script which you have provided. Come to class prepared with the audio portion of a script written out, preferably in handout form. If a handout is not feasible, write the audio portion on the board. Students plan and decide what kinds of visual materials would go well with the narration that has been provided, and where each one would fit into the script. This is done as a class after discussing some possibilities. Be sure that the class understands how to place items in the "visual" column so they correspond with the proper place in the narration (in the "audio" column). One way to get this across is to transcribe a small portion of the narration (audio) from a film and have students fill in the corresponding "visuals" as they watch the film.

HOUR 5: Students create their own practice scripts at their desks. This is done individually; not as a group. The scripts, which should be at least three pages long, describe a "how-to" presentation about a topic which you supply. Choose a simple topic that all students can write about such as "How to Take Care of Your Teeth" or "How to Cook a Specific Food" (popcorn, hamburgers, or the like). Students do not actually make any visual displays or props, but they note the kinds of visuals they would use for the narrations they write. These scripts are handed in to ensure that everyone has a clear idea of how a script is written.

HOUR 6: Each student hands in a research paper about a topic that was studied individually (the class was told during the second hour that their reports would be due at the beginning of this hour). Students must also turn in their notecards and bibliographies for inspection. Be sure to provide enough time (at least a week) between the second and sixth class hours for students to complete their research projects. After the papers are handed in, groups meet to discuss and begin planning their productions. Before the class breaks up into small groups, however, it is helpful to point out the kinds of things groups should be thinking about this hour and Hour 7. Each group needs to decide:

What production or presentation method to use.

The part each person will play in the actual presentation.

Jobs each person can do to prepare for the presentation.

Specific things that will be taught.

Ways to blend everyone's knowledge (from research papers) into a cohesive presentation.

Tell the groups to sit down with their project handouts and discuss what is possible. Hours 6 and 7 are basically a divergent-convergent process where everybody's ideas are listed, even ridiculous ones, and then each idea is discussed to see if it sounds workable or interesting. By Hour 8, when actual scriptwriting begins, groups should have a solid idea of what they want to present and how they will go about it.

HOUR 7: Small groups meet and continue to plan their productions.

HOUR 8: Return research papers, notecards, and bibliographies to students and set a due date for rewritten material. Then have students meet in small groups to share information from their research papers and begin writing scripts and designing visuals.

Note:

• Spend time talking with students about the advantages of planning *simple* backgrounds and props. Encourage them to use their imaginations but not to get too elaborate.

HOURS 9-14: This is the approximate number of hours needed for students to work in small groups developing their productions. You will have to judge if they need additional hours. At the end of the final hour group leaders turn in their production scripts and visuals. Materials must be available during this time for creating visual displays and props.

Note:

- Have ideas and suggestions for final touches ready for members of groups who finish their projects earlier than others. Encourage students to spend all the available time putting *quality* into their work, rather than trying to finish as quickly as possible.

HOUR 15: Return scripts and visuals to group leaders and discuss common problems and ways to improve scripts. Any script improvements that must be made are done this hour. If extensive work is needed, an additional hour should be added before going on to Hour 16.

HOUR 16: Dress rehearsals. Each group goes to a corner of the room, a hallway, the gym, or some other area where its production can be practiced.

HOURS 17-19: Presentations.

HOUR 20: Conduct a final discussion about the skills that were applied in this project and student perceptions about them. What things were learned that might help them study, or prepare presentations in the future? Was it difficult to *plan* and *make decisions* as a group? Were the topics worthwhile? In which areas did they do best, and which could have been improved? Point out to the class that this was probably their first attempt at such a complex project and that first-time efforts are seldom perfect. The experience gained from completing such a process, however, will lead to improved quality in future projects and more confidence in personal ability. Some of the most valuable insights occur at the end of a project as students look back and evaluate what was done. As a teacher, you can greatly increase their insights by pointing out skills developed or benefits gained from the project that they may not have considered.

Note:

- At the end of the hour everyone in the class fills out a "Student Evaluation Sheet." This sheet asks students to evaluate everyone in their small group, as well as themselves, by rating individual performance in ten different areas. These evaluations are handed in and can be used strictly for your own information, or they can be included as part of final grades for this project. The primary function, however, is to give students experience in evaluating their own work.

General Notes About This Project:

- Evaluation sheets for written reports, oral reports, posters, and notecards are provided in the introduction to the Student Research Guide (see

Appendix). This project also offers an excellent opportunity to use the checklists, the "Daily Log," and the blank "Skills Chart" that are supplied in the Student Research Guide.

• You may want to ask a video class at a local high school or college if they are interested in recording your productions on videotape. Such classes are often on the lookout for "subjects" who offer programs that can easily be recorded in a classroom or school studio.

• You may also want to ask other teachers if your students can present their productions for the school or to selected classes.

CLASSROOM PRODUCTIONS
Student Assignment Sheet

The basic purpose of this project is to teach skills: skills that are necessary for independent learning. It is important to know how to *find* information, but it may be even more important to know how to *use* or *present* it. There is no telling what you might need to know in the next 20 years, but it seems a sure thing that having the ability to learn on your own will be a benefit.

"Classroom Productions" is not an easy assignment; your contributions are important throughout the project. You will be working with several other people to plan, make decisions, and give a final presentation. Your group will have the freedom to design a production that is truly unique. This is what makes the project interesting and potentially a lot of fun.

This project will be conducted in small groups (four to six students per group). Each group will select a "leader" and a "secretary." The leader is responsible for seeing that the group works together to complete the requirements of the project. If disagreements arise, the leader settles them; if meetings need to be held, the leader calls them. The leader will insist on quality and make the final decision on questions about the production. Remember, it is not the leader's job to make people behave or participate. Anyone who causes persistent problems will be dealt with by the teacher.

The secretary is responsible for keeping track of what the group is doing, and of all the handouts given to the group. Ideas for the production should be recorded in writing; all rough drafts and a final copy of the group's production script must be kept on file. Each secretary will be given a special notebook for these materials and a file drawer in which to store the notebook. A secretary's notebook should be a record of what the group is doing.

There are a number of other jobs that will need to be filled during the project. Some people may have more than one job, but everyone should have at least one responsibility. This is a list of things that will need to be done:

1. Design and make backgrounds and props.
2. Design and make cue cards, credits, posters, charts, graphs, illustrations, and so forth.
3. Produce a well-written script.
4. Time practice sessions, to be sure the entire presentation does not go over fifteen minutes.
5. Watch television news and/or read newspapers and magazines to collect current news about the topic.
6. If music or other sound effects are to be used, someone should be in charge of figuring out what and how.
7. Someone should be in charge of costumes and makeup (if they are to be used).

COURSE REQUIREMENTS

I. Research

The first assignment is for the group to choose a production topic. Each group member will then select a specific topic to study individually for a written research report. Choose a topic that relates to the group's production topic. Record the information you gather on notecards. These will be handed in, along with the written report and a complete bibliography. In this way each person in the group contributes to the research that is needed to do a project like this. Talk about report topics as a group so that everyone chooses something that fits into the production. Don't have two people research the same topic; that is wasted time and effort. A due date will be set for the research paper.

Written report due date: _____

II. Presentation Methods

Fifteen minutes of class time will be allowed for each presentation. Productions should follow one of these formats. (If your group wants to do something different, have it approved by your teacher first.)

A. A news program, with an anchor person, and reporters.
B. A "60 Minutes" or "20/20" type program, with interviews and investigative reporting.
C. A play which teaches or shows things about the topic.
D. A puppet show.
E. A series of drawings, pictures, or posters that can be used to tell a story or teach a lesson.
F. A round table discussion of "experts."
G. A combination of any or all of these methods.

III. Final Product

The purpose of the project is to produce a 15-minute production that other students could learn from if they watched it carefully. Try to become an *educator* as you work on this project. Make sure that your production is worth showing, by making it a valuable thing for people to see. If other kids can learn from it, it will be worth putting on.

IV. Group Information Chart

Before your group begins working on this project, fill out the following:

GROUP INFORMATION CHART

Group topic:	
NAME	**RESEARCH TOPIC**
Leader:	
Secretary:	
Group member:	
Group member:	
Group member:	
Group member:	

Name _____ Date _____

CHOOSING A TOPIC

In choosing a topic your group has three options:

1. Choose one of the topics on this handout and concentrate on the list of questions given.
2. Choose your own topic. For this, your group will turn in a list of at least ten questions that will be answered, subjects that will be explained, or issues that will be covered.
3. Choose one of the topics on this handout but create your own set of questions, subjects, or issues, and turn them in for approval.

It is not necessary to answer *all* of the questions or cover *all* of the issues on the list, but at least *think* about them. Each person in your group will choose one very specific topic to write a research paper about. Notecards are required.

I. THE MIDDLE EAST

1. Identify the countries and the leaders.
2. Use maps to show where these countries are located in the world and where they are located in relation to one another.
3. Explain the formation of Israel as a Jewish state.
4. Describe the wars between Israel and its Arab neighbors since 1948.
5. Try to explain why the Arab nations seem to be determined not to make any compromises with Israel, and vice versa.
6. Try to explain why there is so much pressure in Israel to keep all or most of the conquered Arab land.
7. Why is the United States so interested in the Middle East?
8. Why is Jerusalem such a controversial city?
9. Describe some of the ancient history of the Middle East.
10. Explain what the Camp David Summit was.
11. Report on current events in the Middle East, such as recent events in Lebanon or Iran or Israel or Syria or Iraq or any other Middle East country.
12. Why is oil an important Middle East topic?

II. THE ECONOMY: PRICES, TAXES, INTEREST RATES, BUDGET DEFICITS, AND UNEMPLOYMENT

1. Explain "inflation" by giving a definition and a few good examples to make the definition clear. Do the same for "interest rate," "unemployment," and "budget deficit."

CHOOSING A TOPIC (continued)

2. Describe some of the things that make inflation get worse.
3. Make a comparison between prices today and those of 5, 10, 25, and 50 years ago.
4. Gather the opinions of others with a questionnaire about taxes and budget deficits.
5. How are interest rates related to the federal budget?
6. What would you do to stop unemployment if you were president of the United States? How would you balance the budget?
7. How does inflation in America affect other countries? How about interest rates?
8. Explain what a "depression" is, and describe the Great Depression of the 1930s.
9. Make graphs which show how inflation has increased or decreased over the past few years. Do the same for interest rates and the federal deficit.
10. Write letters to well-known economists to ask for opinions about inflation, interest rates, unemployment, or the federal deficit.
11. Interview your parents and grandparents about federal and state spending, taxes, and deficits.
12. Explain how the stock market works.

III. ENVIRONMENTAL POLLUTION

1. Describe what basic things human beings need to comfortably live healthy lives.
2. Explain how these things can become polluted.
3. Explain the history of pollution, beginning with sewage problems in ancient cities, and continuing to the new problems created by the modern world.
4. What kinds of things are polluting our environment today? How do they hurt people?
5. Is anybody doing anything about pollution? Find out who is and write letters to them.
6. Watch the news and record every instance of environmental pollution that is reported.
7. What are the future dangers of pollution?
8. Where can pollution be found in our environment? Give examples.
9. How does pollution affect the wild animals and natural areas of the world? Give examples.
10. What is "acid rain"? What should be done about it?
11. Explain how radioactive pollution can occur and what its effects are.

IV. SELF-SUFFICIENT LIVING

1. What does "self-sufficient living" mean?
2. Explain what an organic garden is and what kinds of things can be grown in one.
3. Describe three or four ways of preserving food without using electricity.
4. Using diagrams and models, show how a log cabin can be built, and what materials are needed.
5. Explain how solar energy can be used to reduce electric and oil bills.
6. Explain the importance of knowing how to use tools, make repairs, and build things that are needed around the house. Also include sewing, weaving, and cooking.
7. Describe what a self-sufficient household would be like. Is it possible for people to be totally self-sufficient? What are the limits?
8. Why is it important to even *think* about being self-sufficient?
9. Make a list of skills a person should have if he/she wants to be self-sufficient.
10. Do demonstrations to show specific skills such as building fires, making candles or soap, constructing a machine, or working with cloth.

CHOOSING A TOPIC (continued)
V. THE ATOMIC AGE

1. Explain what an "atomic reaction" is, and how energy is released from such a reaction.
2. Explain what the "Manhattan Project" was and why it was necessary.
3. What happened at Hiroshima that began the atomic age?
4. Describe the relationship between the U.S. and the U.S.S.R. since the discovery of the atomic bomb.
5. Make a graph showing the yearly increase in atomic weapons in the world since 1945.
6. On a world map show all the countries which now possess atomic weapons, and also those which will have them in the next five years or so.
7. Explain how atomic energy is used during peacetime.
8. What are the advantages and disadvantages of using atomic energy in America?
9. How is atomic waste from reactors disposed of?
10. What are the ecological hazards of atomic reactors? How do present reactors affect their environments?
11. Write to the power company to get an explanation of its position on the issue of using atomic energy to generate electricity; send letters to any other organizations that can give you further information.

VI. THE SPACE AGE

1. What was "Sputnik"?
2. How did Sputnik change attitudes in America about space exploration?
3. Describe our space program in general, from the first satellite to the present day.
4. Describe the Apollo program in some detail. Use models or diagrams.
5. Why do we want to get into space? What good is the space program?
6. Describe the space shuttle, and make a brief time-line of its history.
7. Why is there competition between the U.S. and the U.S.S.R. in space exploration and technology?
8. Explain some of the history of astronomy and some of the old theories that have been proven wrong.
9. Choose a topic about the space program and explain it thoroughly.
10. Choose a topic from astronomy (super novas, comets, black holes, the speed of light, and so forth) and explain it as well as you can.
11. What is "Star Wars"?
12. When will the first space station be built, and what will it look like?
13. Discuss the crises, accidents, and other setbacks that the U.S. space program has experienced over the years.
14. How much has the space program cost each year? Compare these figures.

VII. ENDANGERED SPECIES

1. Define "endangered species."
2. Make a list of endangered animals in the world.
3. Use maps to show where the last members of endangered species live (other than zoos). You may also make a "Major Zoos" map to show where endangered animals are being preserved.
4. Why have certain species become endangered?
5. Pick three or four endangered species and do a study of them: Where does each species fit into its food web? Are they predator or prey animals? What has caused each species to decline in numbers? Can they be saved? What would have to be done to save them? What are their natural habitats?

6. Interview an expert or professional about endangered species, and find out what role zoos play in helping these animals.

7. Write letters to people, groups, organizations, zoos, and government agencies that are interested in endangered species.

8. Build models and/or make posters that show an endangered species in its natural habitat, and also in an environment disturbed by humans.

9. What can people who are concerned about endangered species do to help them?

10. Are humans the only reason there are endangered species of animals?

VIII. CURRENT EVENTS IN THE WORLD

1. Use maps to show the areas of the world you are reporting about.

2. Collect headlines from the newspapers to introduce your stories.

3. Explain what "unemployment" is and why it concerns so many people in America. Do the same for "budget deficit."

4. Describe what is taking place between Israel and the Arab countries of the Middle East. What is happening between the Arab countries themselves?

5. Explain why the Soviets are so interested in Poland and Afghanistan, and what the Soviet influence in these countries means to America.

6. Make a chart that shows the value of the American dollar compared with other currencies of the world, especially the Japanese yen, the German mark, and the Mexican peso.

7. Why is chemical pollution becoming such a problem?

8. What is "terrorism," and why is it being used in the world today?

9. Describe the space program, and explain what kinds of things it will be doing in the future.

10. Who are some of the important leaders in today's world?

11. What are the causes of famine and where is it occurring in the world?

12. Remember: Current events change. You may want to make a new list of events to study.

IX. ENVIRONMENTAL CURRENT EVENTS

1. Explain what "ecology" is. How is the ecology of the world being upset?

2. What is done with nuclear waste in the United States?

3. What has been discovered about asbestos and people who live or work around it?

4. Explain what "forestry" is and why trees are important to the modern world as well as to the pioneer.

5. Describe the process of human expansion in the United States and what that has done to wildlife and to the environment itself.

6. How can we capture energy from the sun to replace our dwindling supply of oil? What other pollution-free sources of energy are there?

7. Write letters to the Environmental Protection Agency, the Sierra Club, the Department of Natural Resources, the Audubon Society, The National Park Service, the National Rifle Association, the National Wildlife Federation, and so forth, and ask for information about environmental issues.

8. Why is there so much interest in organic gardening? How do pesticides, herbicides, and fertilizers pollute the environment?

9. Who is the current Secretary of the Interior? What do environmentalists think about him or her? What do business people think about his or her policies?

10. What is "acid rain"?

11. Remember: Current events change. You may want to make a new list of events to study.

Name _____ Date _____

PRESENTATION METHODS

Now that your group has chosen a topic, decide how to present it so that it is interesting and educational. Remember, the presentation will *teach* factual information; kids your own age should be able to *learn* something by watching it. There are a number of ways to produce such a presentation. Maybe your group has already decided how to present its topic. If so, you should still read this handout carefully for ideas, hints, and requirements.

I. PRODUCTION REQUIREMENTS

A. Produce an accurate and well-written script that describes the production step-by-step. The script will be handed in.

B. The presentation must be educational; it should answer several of the questions provided on the topic selection handout, or present other facts that have been discovered through research. Decide what facts and ideas to teach and then create a presentation that actually teaches those things.

C. The presentation cannot be more than 15 minutes long (this includes time for setting up, changing props and sets, and so forth).

II. PRODUCTION METHODS

A. A "News Broadcast" Format. Have someone be the "anchor person" (like on the evening news) to introduce stories. Then the scene can switch to special reporters. These reporters will interview people, show drawings, charts, or diagrams and explain them, or do demonstrations. Someone can also give an editorial comment. Behind the anchor person there can be a display of maps, pictures, headlines, and the like. Don't forget to point to pictures or drawings as they are discussed, because you don't have a camera zooming in on details as they have on television. The anchor person can also describe quick news stories while facing the audience. There are many things that can be done with charts, graphs, and pictures in front of the audience while the anchor person is talking from the side.

II. PRODUCTION METHODS (continued)

B. A "60 Minutes" Format. This method is mostly interview and calls for a bit of acting. Decide on a very specific topic, and then "interview" famous people about that topic. For instance, students could interview specific Middle East and U.S. leaders for a "60 Minutes" report on the Middle East. Another way to use this method is to interview fictional (make-believe) people, and have them give information in their answers. For instance, an interview might be conducted with Dr. Hans Schweikendorf (completely fictional person) about what he has seen through his telescope, followed by an attempt to prove that what he has seen is possible (or impossible) by interviewing other fictional "experts." The things these people say, of course, must be accurate information. You can also include a short debate between people who disagree about the topic being presented.

C. A "Puppet Show" Format. For a puppet show to become a good presentation, a lot of time must be spent making sets, writing conversations, and making puppets. Be very careful that the information you are trying to present is clear: will the audience understand what you are teaching? Beyond these requirements, the puppet show format is fairly open. You are free to create characters, plot, and setting. If suggestions are needed, try some of these:

1. A classroom setting with a teacher giving information to a class, or students asking questions, making reports, having conversations, and so forth.

2. Friends talking among themselves.

3. A re-creation of an actual historical event, like the landing on the moon.

4. A demonstration, such as puppet characters planting an organic garden and using solar energy.

5. A drama, with characters that are involved in, or affected by, something (such as a forest fire, a polluted river, a war, or the economy). These characters don't have to be famous people, and in fact, they don't even need to be human beings.

D. A "Play" Format. A play is like a puppet show, except that the parts are played by humans instead of puppets. Think carefully about sets, cue cards, costumes, and what is to be taught. Read the outline for a puppet show format to get additional ideas for your play. Remember that the entire play will take place in the front of the classroom and last no more than fifteen minutes.

E. A "Picture-narration" Format. This method is something like making a cartoon. Draw a series of pictures and write a narration to go with them. Then, as the audience looks at the pictures, tell a story. The pictures, combined with the narration, *teach* something. Pictures from magazines and books can be used but they should be fairly large so the audience can see them. Use your own drawings as much as possible.

F. Other. If your group comes up with a presentation method that is not mentioned, that's great! Have your idea checked first, though, to help ensure that it will work.

Once a production method is decided upon, it is time to actually begin putting together a show. The secretary should keep track of the ideas and decisions made by the group as the production is designed. Remember to keep the props, costumes, and presentation outline simple so that your group's time can be used to produce a show that is well-organized and easily understood by the audience. Details can always be added to a basic plan, whereas it is more difficult to simplify complex ideas that aren't working.

Name _____ Date _____

STUDENT EVALUATION SHEET

List the people in your group (including yourself) on the spaces across the top of this page. As fairly and honestly as you can, give each person an evaluation for the ten categories itemized in the left-hand column. Circle a number for each category under each group member's name: "1" is poor, "5" is excellent.

GROUP MEMBERS' NAMES

Evaluation Categories _____ | _____ | _____ | _____ | _____ | _____

Category					
1. Total contribution to the project	1 2 3 4 5	1 2 3 4 5	1 2 3 4 5	1 2 3 4 5	1 2 3 4 5
2. Sharing ideas	1 2 3 4 5	1 2 3 4 5	1 2 3 4 5	1 2 3 4 5	1 2 3 4 5
3. Accepting others' ideas	1 2 3 4 5	1 2 3 4 5	1 2 3 4 5	1 2 3 4 5	1 2 3 4 5
4. Concentrating on the project	1 2 3 4 5	1 2 3 4 5	1 2 3 4 5	1 2 3 4 5	1 2 3 4 5
5. Taking care of materials	1 2 3 4 5	1 2 3 4 5	1 2 3 4 5	1 2 3 4 5	1 2 3 4 5
6. Effort	1 2 3 4 5	1 2 3 4 5	1 2 3 4 5	1 2 3 4 5	1 2 3 4 5
7. Willingness to work	1 2 3 4 5	1 2 3 4 5	1 2 3 4 5	1 2 3 4 5	1 2 3 4 5
8. Quality of work	1 2 3 4 5	1 2 3 4 5	1 2 3 4 5	1 2 3 4 5	1 2 3 4 5
9. General attitude	1 2 3 4 5	1 2 3 4 5	1 2 3 4 5	1 2 3 4 5	1 2 3 4 5
10. Organization and neatness	1 2 3 4 5	1 2 3 4 5	1 2 3 4 5	1 2 3 4 5	1 2 3 4 5

TOTAL
(50 pts. possible) _____ _____ _____ _____ _____

BOOK REPORTS

Teacher Preview

General Explanation:
This project is designed to be done entirely on the student's own time. Each student is to complete six book reports over the course of a school year. Emphasis is placed on self-discipline, meeting deadlines, and making progress in other independent learning skills, along with following the assignment outline and basic writing skills.

Length of Project: 2 hours

Level of Independence: Advanced

Goals:

1. To encourage students to read and to improve their reading skills.
2. To place emphasis on independent learning through reading.

During This Project Students Will:

1. Read books from various categories.
2. Write book reports using proper writing skills.
3. Meet deadlines independently.

Skills:

Summarizing	Meeting deadlines
Grammar	Accepting responsibility
Handwriting	Individualized study habits
Neatness	Time management
Paragraphs	Personal motivation
Sentences	Sense of "quality"
Spelling	Creative expression
Organizing	Following project outlines
Selecting topics	Writing

Handouts Provided:

- "Student Assignment Sheet"
- "Book Report Record Sheet"

PROJECT CALENDAR:

HOUR 1: _____	HOUR 2: _____	HOUR 3: _____
Students are given the assignment and record sheets; discussion of book reports and the importance of meeting deadlines. Due dates are given and recorded on record sheets. HANDOUTS PROVIDED	Book reports are turned in on dates specified during Hour 1. STUDENTS TURN IN WORK	
HOUR 4: _____	HOUR 5: _____	HOUR 6: _____
HOUR 7: _____	HOUR 8: _____	HOUR 9: _____

Lesson Plans and Notes

HOUR 1: Distribute the "Book Reports" assignment sheet, which explains what kinds of books the students are required to read as well as how to write a book report. Establish a time-line with six due dates (the handout calls for a book report on each of six different kinds of books). You can set up the time-line in several different ways:

1. Designate one date as the final date by which all six reports must be turned in, for instance, the day before spring break. Reports should be handed in as they are completed over the course of the year.

2. Designate two or three dates during the year when a few of the reports are due. For instance, two reports might be due on November 15, two on February 1, and two on April 15.

3. Designate separate due dates for the reports, spaced at intervals of two to five weeks.

Also give students the second handout, "Book Report Record Sheet." Students record the due dates on this sheet. In addition, they record the titles of books as they are read, the categories they are from, and the dates the book reports are completed. There is also a place for recording the grades received. Book reports are graded for writing mechanics, proper form, and whether they were turned in on time. Students who are not accustomed to assignments with long-range due dates should be given specific dates for each report or at least for the first two or three.

HOUR 2: Book reports are turned in on dates specified during Hour 1.

General Notes About This Project:

- Written book reports should be carefully graded for basic writing and language skills.

- It is a good idea to provide a reading list from which students can select books if they wish. Students should show you the books they have selected if you have never heard of them. Require students to read *quality* literature.

- You may add a wide variety of book report categories to the handout that is provided. The emphasis of this handout is on topical subjects and nonfiction. The original idea was to encourage students to read books about topics they were studying in other classes.

- It is left to the teacher to determine a page minimum for the books being read. It is advisable to set such a minimum to prevent certain students from reading very simple or very short books.

Name _____ Date _____

BOOK REPORTS
Student Assignment Sheet

Reading and writing are age-old activities. Just as writing is the key to sharing thoughts with others, reading is a way of discovering what others have to say. Books contain the thoughts of people who have taken the time to put their ideas into words. The only way to discover these ideas is to *read*.

Book reports are a way of ensuring that students read books, while giving you the freedom to choose your own reading material (within limits). The ability to read a book and report on it independently is an indication that a student can learn on his or her own. Be intelligent in your selection of books. Choose titles, stories, or authors that are of interest or that meet an academic need (such as reading a book about Abraham Lincoln while you are studying the Civil War in history class). Above all, use this assignment for self-education: learn everything possible from the books while improving your ability to write a book report.

You will be required to do at least six book reports this year. Each report will be about a different category of book, but you may choose to read the categories in any order; for example, your first report might be about a nature book, followed by a biography, and so on. These are the six categories:

_____ 1. ANIMALS or PLANTS: This book can be about a certain species (like Siberian tigers or sugar maple trees), or a more general group (like cats or trees).

_____ 2. BIOGRAPHY or AUTOBIOGRAPHY: Read a book that tells the story of someone who really lived.

_____ 3. PIONEERS or INDIANS: Read a book that tells about pioneer days or that tells about Indians and how they lived. The book can be fiction or nonfiction, but the main story must be about the early days of America.

_____ 4. SCIENCE FICTION or FANTASY: Read a book that is imaginary and deals in some way with science, the future, or fantasy.

_____ 5. NATURE: This book can be about such things as astronomy, geology, weather, gardening, volcanoes, earthquakes, oceanography, forestry, ecology, the environment, chemistry, hurricanes, deserts, mountains, glaciers, energy from the sun, and so forth. It should *not* be about animals or plants, since these forms of nature are covered in book report category one.

_____ 6. HISTORY: This book can be fiction or nonfiction, but it should be about some period of history other than pioneer days, which is covered by book report category three. Some possible periods of history are: the Roman Empire, the Dark Ages, the Stone Age, the Middle Ages, the Civil War, the Second World War, the Great Depression, the Wild West (following the Civil War), ancient Egypt, the history of any country, the American Revolution (the war itself, not pioneer stories), and so forth.

BOOK REPORTS (continued)

Hand your book reports in on or before the dates they are due. Use the spaces next to each number on this handout to check off the reports as you finish them. Book reports should be written on lined paper in your neatest handwriting. Use complete sentences and correct spelling, punctuation, capitalization, grammar, and paragraphs.

Use this general outline to help organize each book report:

I. Bibliography

    A. The type of book you are writing about (animals or plants, biography or autobiography, science fiction or fantasy, nature, pioneers or Indians, history).

    B. The title of the book.

    C. The author of the book.

    D. Who published the book.

    E. When it was copyrighted.

    F. How many pages it has.

II. Book Summary

    A. Write a two- to three-page description of the book that could be used to help other people decide if it is the kind of book they want to read. Do not give your opinions here!

        1. Describe how the book presented information. Was it a story or a book of information? How was it organized?

        2. What topics did it cover?

        3. If the book was fiction, describe these parts of the story:

            a. Characters

            b. Setting

            c. Plot

        4. If the book was nonfiction, what kind of information was in each chapter? Provide enough details so that it is clear you understand what the book was about.

        5. Explain why someone would read the book (enjoyment, research, general knowledge or in-depth information about a specific topic). Why did *you* choose this book?

    B. In one or two paragraphs, explain what you learned or gained from reading the book.

        1. Did the characters have certain traits that you liked?

        2. What facts did it present that you didn't know before?

        3. Did it spark an interest in any new subjects?

        4. Did it explain things so you understood them better?

        5. Did you learn any new words?

        6. Was the author trying to teach a lesson, make a point, present factual information, or just entertain you?

        7. Could reading this book help you become a better writer? How?

III. Personal Opinion

    A. In one or two paragraphs explain how you feel about the book.

        1. Did you enjoy the book? Why or why not?

        2. Was it written so you could understand it?

        3. What made this book easy or difficult to read?

        4. Did you like the way the author wrote the book?

        5. What part was most interesting to you?

        6. What part was least interesting to you?

        7. Would you read another book by the same author?

        8. What other praises or criticisms do you have for the book?

    B. Would you advise someone else to read this book? Explain your answer: why would you give this advice?

Name _____ Date _____

BOOK REPORT RECORD SHEET

This page will become a record of your book reports for this school year. Record the due date for each report in the spaces below. Remember that the categories can be read in any order: book report number one can be about pioneers, nature, history, or any of the other categories. Read one book from each category, and turn in a report on or before the due date.

Book Report Number	Due Date
1	_____
2	_____
3	_____
4	_____
5	_____
6	_____

Fill in the blanks below as book reports are completed. This is your record of the project, and it should be kept safely in a notebook. You may be required to hand it in with your book reports so that grades can be recorded on it. If so, it will be returned with each graded report.

	Title	Category	Date Completed	Grade
1.	_____ _____	_____	_____	_____
2.	_____ _____	_____	_____	_____
3.	_____ _____	_____	_____	_____
4.	_____ _____	_____	_____	_____
5.	_____ _____	_____	_____	_____
6.	_____ _____	_____	_____	_____

CLASS NEWSPAPER

Teacher Preview

General Explanation:
This project is designed primarily as an independent writing project: students are given a handout and a set of due dates. Each time one part of the assignment is due, an hour is spent explaining the requirements of the next part. At the end, small groups develop specific sections for a class newspaper. A project time-line is provided following the Lesson Plans and Notes.

Length of Project: 16 hours

Level of Independence: Advanced

Goals:

1. To allow students to write about a wide variety of issues.

2. To promote the concept of "kids teaching kids."

3. To provide a forum where students can express their points of view.

During This Project Students Will:

1. Assemble information for newspaper articles.

2. Write news articles.

3. Write editorials.

4. Create cartoons or comic strips.

5. Develop advertising strategies.

6. Plan a complete school newspaper.

Skills:

Preparing bibliographies	Grammar
Collecting data	Handwriting
Interviewing	Neatness
Library skills	Paragraphs
Summarizing	Sentences
Spelling	Persistence
Organizing	Time management
Selecting topics	Personal motivation
Following project outlines	Sense of "quality"

Meeting deadlines	Creative expression
Accepting responsibility	Teaching others
Individualized study habits	Group planning
Working with others	Writing

Handouts Provided:

- "Student Assignment Sheet"
- Student Research Guide (optional; see Appendix)
  a. "Daily Log"
  b. "Blank Skills Chart"
  c. "Bibliographies"
  d. "Notecards and Bibliographies"

PROJECT CALENDAR:

HOUR 1: _____	HOUR 2: _____	HOUR 3: _____
Review of the parts of a newspaper; examples are read to the class.	Assignment sheet is handed out; due dates are set and recorded on assignment sheets. Each student will produce six different types of written material by the end of Hour 9.	Discussion of news items from newspapers. A method of developing a news article is explained. Students will hand in news articles next hour.
PREPARATION REQUIRED	HANDOUT PROVIDED	PREPARATION REQUIRED
HOUR 4: _____	**HOUR 5:** _____	**HOUR 6:** _____
Students hand in their news articles, followed by a discussion of topics and ideas for articles about school. Students will hand in school articles next hour.	School articles are handed in, followed by a discussion of general interest articles found in newspapers. Students will hand in general interest articles next hour.	General interest articles are turned in, followed by a discussion of advertising in newspapers. Students will hand in advertisements next hour.
STUDENTS TURN IN WORK PREPARATION REQUIRED	STUDENTS TURN IN WORK PREPARATION REQUIRED	STUDENTS TURN IN WORK PREPARATION REQUIRED
HOUR 7: _____	**HOUR 8:** _____	**HOUR 9:** _____
Advertisements are turned in, followed by a discussion of cartoons and comics. Students will hand in cartoons and comics next hour.	Cartoons and comics are turned in, followed by a discussion of newspaper editorials. Students will hand in editorials next hour.	Editorials are turned in, followed by a discussion of the class newspaper: how it will be organized, who will produce it, and when it will be published.
STUDENTS TURN IN WORK PREPARATION REQUIRED	STUDENTS TURN IN WORK PREPARATION REQUIRED	STUDENTS TURN IN WORK PREPARATION REQUIRED

PROJECT CALENDAR (continued):

HOUR 10: _____	HOUR 11: _____	HOUR 12: _____
Graded materials are returned, small groups are formed, and the process of producing a newspaper is begun. RETURN STUDENT WORK	Small groups work on their sections of the newspaper.	Students work in groups.
HOUR 13: _____	HOUR 14: _____	HOUR 15: _____
Students work in groups.	Students work in groups.	Newspaper material is put into its final form and turned in at the end of the hour. STUDENTS TURN IN WORK
HOUR 16: _____	HOUR 17: _____	HOUR 18: _____
Newspaper pages are collated and stapled, followed by a discussion of the ways that independent learning skills were used in this project. PREPARATION REQUIRED		

Lesson Plans and Notes

HOUR 1: Spend this hour reviewing the parts of a newspaper. Read to the class examples of news, local events, and general interest articles as well as several cartoons, advertisements, and editorials.

HOUR 2: Distribute the "Student Assignment Sheet" and explain it point-by-point. At the end of the hour students will understand the basics of the six separate writing assignments, and the due date for each. They may begin work on these assignments immediately, but be prepared to provide further classroom explanation and clarification of each succeeding assignment on the day that something is due. In other words, set aside one hour on each due date for discussion of the next assignment. Be sure to set due dates so that students have enough time to complete assignments *and* you have enough time to grade them. (A time-line is provided following the lesson plans as an example of a workable schedule.)

HOUR 3: During this hour discuss international, national, state, and local news stories from newspapers while focusing on Part 1 of the assignment sheet. Emphasize the need for research and explain the following method of developing a news article: gather the information, organize it, summarize it, and write it into one informative article. The assigned article is due at the beginning of Hour 4. Each student chooses a news area and one topic to write about. Give students at least one week to complete the assignment.

HOUR 4: Students hand in their news articles. Then spend the hour discussing how to choose a topic, gather information, and prepare an article about school (Part II of the assignment sheet). This article is due at the beginning of Hour 5. Give students at least one week to complete the assignment.

HOUR 5: Students hand in school articles. Spend the hour discussing the wide variety of general interest topics that can be found in a newspaper (Part III of the assignment sheet). Students choose an *area* and then a *specific topic;* their articles are due at the beginning of Hour 6. Give students at least one week to complete the assignment.

HOUR 6: Students hand in articles assigned during Hour 5. Spend the hour discussing advertising in newspapers (Part IV of the assignment sheet). Students' advertisements are due at the beginning of Hour 7. Give students at least two days to complete the assignment.

HOUR 7: Advertisements are handed in. Spend the hour discussing cartoons and comics in newspapers (Part V of the assignment sheet). Cartoons or comics must be turned in at the beginning of Hour 8. Give students at least two days to complete the assignment.

HOUR 8: Cartoons and comics are handed in. Spend the hour discussing newspaper editorials (Part VI of the assignment sheet). Editorials must be turned in at the beginning of Hour 9. Give students at least one week to complete the assignment.

HOUR 9: Editorials are turned in. Spend the hour discussing the production of a class newspaper: how it will be structured, the method of forming small groups (Hour 10), the responsibilities of each person within a group, and what the name of the newspaper will be.

HOUR 10: All graded materials are handed back; some material may have already been returned, but you must have everything back in students' hands by this hour. This hour ends the *writing* project and from here on the project consists of *constructing* a student or school newspaper. Although there are a number of ways to organize the production of a class newspaper, here is one that works well:

1. Divide the class into six groups (four to six students per group).

2. In a class discussion (Hour 10) decide how much material should be included in each section: discuss the relative difficulty of each category and come to a class consensus of what is fair. These decisions, made by the class, determine the size of the newspaper and the extent of each section. Limits on time and materials should be taken into account.

3. Assign each group a section of the paper to develop: there are six categories of writing in the project, and each one becomes a section of the paper.

4. Have students give their graded written material to the appropriate group: news stories go to the group working on the news section of the paper, comics go to the comics group, and so forth.

5. Students work in class to select material and complete their sections of the newspaper. When finished, each group turns in its section, written in reproducible form (either handwritten or typed).

6. Pages are duplicated.

7. Pages are collated and stapled.

8. Newspapers are distributed.

Notes:

- Other options for creating a newspaper: (1) assign a small group of "editors" the job of selecting material for a class newspaper; (2) have *each* student create a mini-newspaper from his or her own work; or (3) have small groups of two, three, or four students combine their work into a collection of newspapers: each group produces its own unique paper. There are, obviously, many variations of the uses you can make of student articles and other materials once they are written.

- Be aware that some children will be sensitive about having their graded material seen by other students. You can alleviate this problem greatly by telling students early on that material will be shared in groups. In an "advanced" project like this, however, students should be expected to respect the work and feelings of others in the class.

HOUR 11: In groups, students work on their sections of the newspaper. It is important to stress brevity, conciseness, and editorial control over the length of articles. There is a danger that the newspaper will become too large to be practical. Not all of the material that was produced during the project can be included, so each group's first responsibility is to reduce the available material by reading it and selecting what is considered the best work. Portions of articles can also be used if the "editors" feel that they are well written and serve a specific purpose.

HOURS 12-14: Students work in groups.

HOUR 15: Students put their newspaper material into final form and turn it in at the end of the hour. This material must be ready to be duplicated since no more work will be done on it; it is a good idea to proofread everything before duplicating it.

HOUR 16: The newspaper is collated and stapled. (Newspaper material must be duplicated before this hour.) Spend the remainder of the hour discussing the ways that higher level thinking and independent learning skills were employed during this project. The blank skills chart provided in the Student Research Guide can be used at this time. Students look at the list of subskills and discuss how each applied (or did not apply, as the case may be) to the project. Emphasis is placed on the universal value of these skills: they are common ingredients in almost any independent learning situation.

General Notes About This Project:

- Before beginning this project, it may be a good idea to provide a newspaper unit for your class to more thoroughly cover the sections of a newspaper and the types of writing used in most general circulation papers.

- The Student Research Guide offers a "Daily Log" that is useful for having students keep track of their out-of-class work. The blank skills chart is also helpful when talking about the value of independent learning skills in a project like this: students can chart skills as they are used, and these charts can serve as the basis for the classroom discussion during Hour 16.

- This project is designed to produce the highest quality newspaper possible using material from the entire class, but it means that some kids may end up not having anything chosen for the class paper. If you prefer to publish something from everyone, then you may want to use one of the options discussed in the first note under HOUR 10.

CLASS NEWSPAPER TIME LINE

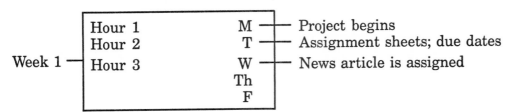

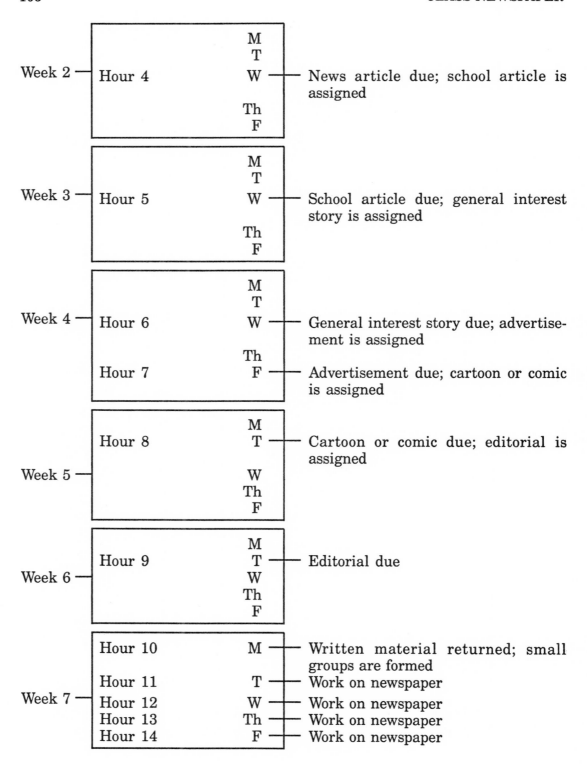

Week 2 — Hour 4 —
M
T
W — News article due; school article is assigned
Th
F

Week 3 — Hour 5 —
M
T
W — School article due; general interest story is assigned
Th
F

Week 4 — Hour 6 —
M
T
W — General interest story due; advertisement is assigned
Th
Hour 7 — F — Advertisement due; cartoon or comic is assigned

Week 5 — Hour 8 —
M
T — Cartoon or comic due; editorial is assigned
W
Th
F

Week 6 — Hour 9 —
M
T — Editorial due
W
Th
F

Week 7 —
Hour 10 — M — Written material returned; small groups are formed
Hour 11 — T — Work on newspaper
Hour 12 — W — Work on newspaper
Hour 13 — Th — Work on newspaper
Hour 14 — F — Work on newspaper

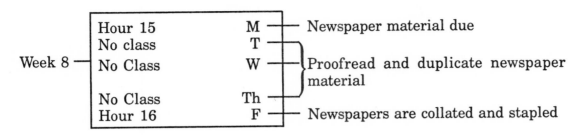

CLASS NEWSPAPER
Student Assignment Sheet

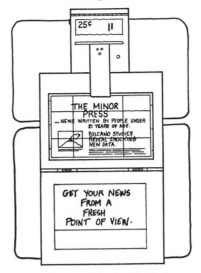

Producing a newspaper is an interesting and challenging way to exercise writing skills. It requires research, planning, problem solving, self-discipline and self-evaluation skills, as well as the ability to write. This project places great importance on these skills because they apply to almost any independent undertaking you can think of. Publishing a newspaper is a good way to practice them.

There is, of course, one other vital skill for independent learning: presentation. In other words—the ability to display, exhibit, show, present, or use what has been produced. You are going to write material for a newspaper, and your class will actually publish a newspaper. This is your presentation. It is your work, and it should be done with as much quality as possible. Each student becomes a reporter/editor/advertiser/writer/cartoonist for the paper, making a number of contributions on a variety of topics. Here is the assignment.

I. Write a news article about any topic you choose from one of the four areas listed below:
    A. International (anywhere in the world except America)
    B. National (American news)
    C. State (news from your home state)
    D. Local (news from your home town)

This article will require *research!* Choose a topic and start collecting information from newspapers, magazines, and television. Inform yourself before writing a news article. Prepare a bibliography of news sources.

II. Write a school article about any topic you choose. Some examples are given below:
    A. Teacher interview
    B. Student profiles
    C. PTA activities
    D. Music or art programs
    E. School history (interview old-timers such as retired teachers or people who went to the school years ago)
    F. School programs and activities
    G. Parent interviews
    H. Classroom activities
    I. Sports

CLASS NEWSPAPER (continued)

III. Write an article about one of the following general interest topics. (General interest means it must be factual but it is written primarily because people are interested in the topic rather than because something important has happened.)

A. Sports
B. Fine arts (music, dance, sculpture, painting, acting, and so forth)
C. Cooking and food
D. Fashion
E. Science
F. Politics
G. Movies
H. Travel
I. Modern living
J. Consumer report

This article will also require some research. Since research time is limited, be sure to choose a topic that you already know something about, and check yourself by looking things up; *all information must be accurate!* Prepare a bibliography of information sources.

IV. Make up an advertisement that can be run in the newspaper. It may be humorous, but don't make it ridiculous. Pretend that you own a store and sell things that people your age buy. Think of some way to get them to buy from *you.* Maybe you can think of something *real* to advertise like a local garage sale or a fund raiser or a school dance. If so, use it!

V. Create a cartoon or comic strip for the newspaper. It can be a political cartoon or one that is just humorous. What is done with this part of the assignment is up to you, as long as some kind of original cartoon or comic strip is turned in.

VI. Write an editorial about something you believe in strongly. This can be about anything from student rights to energy conservation to parent problems. Write to convince others that your point of view is correct and that they should join in your beliefs, or at least be sympathetic to them.

Each assignment will be turned in on the date assigned in class. Record these dates on the spaces below. The lengths of the articles will vary, but all should be at least one page of neat, single-spaced handwriting. After everything is graded (and rewritten, if necessary), the class will begin organizing material into a newspaper. This portion of the assignment will be explained by the teacher.

DUE DATES

1. News article _____

2. School article _____

3. General interest article _____

4. Advertisement _____

5. Cartoon or comic strip _____

6. Editorial _____

RESEARCH/REPORT PROJECTS

Teacher Preview

Project Topics: The Fifty States of America
Foreign Countries
The World of Science
Inventions and Discoveries

General Explanation:

These four research projects are virtually identical in structure, but each emphasizes a distinctly different subject area. They are designed as independent projects, requiring only four class hours each. However, they can easily be restructured as classroom or library research projects, in which case they each require approximately fifteen class hours. A student self-evaluation form that can be used with any of the projects is provided; it follows the last assignment sheet ("Inventions and Discoveries").

Length of Each Project: 4 hours

Level of Independence: Advanced

Goals:

1. To require the use of research skills as students learn about specific topics.

2. To place emphasis on writing as the primary focus of a research project.

3. To place emphasis on independent learning.

During This Project Students Will:

1. Choose topics for research.

2. Assemble information for reports.

3. Prepare proper bibliographies.

4. Write correct outlines.

5. Produce properly written reports.

Skills:

Preparing bibliographies	Divergent-convergent-evaluative thinking
Collecting data	Following project outlines
Writing letters	Identifying problems
Library skills	Meeting deadlines
Making notecards	Accepting responsibility

Summarizing	Concentration
Grammar	Controlling behavior
Handwriting	Individualized study habits
Neatness	Persistence
Paragraphs	Time management
Sentences	Personal motivation
Spelling	Sense of "quality"
Organizing	Setting personal goals
Outlining	Creative expression
Setting objectives	Self-confidence
Selecting topics	Writing

Handouts Provided:

- "Student Assignment Sheet" for each area of study
- "Student Self-Evaluation Sheet"
- Teacher's Introduction to the Student Research Guide (optional; see Appendix)
  a. "Notecard Evaluation"
  b. "Writing Evaluation"
- Student Research Guide (optional; see Appendix)
  a. Choose handouts that meet your needs.

PROJECT CALENDAR:

HOUR 1:	HOUR 2:	HOUR 3:
Assignment sheets are handed out, the project is discussed and due dates are given.	Students turn in notecards, bibliographies, and outlines. Discussion of research problems, discoveries, and questions.	Notecards, bibliographies, and outlines are returned; discussion of common problems or errors in producing these materials. Students ask questions about their grades.
HANDOUTS PROVIDED	STUDENTS TURN IN WORK	RETURN STUDENT WORK
HOUR 4:	**HOUR 5:**	**HOUR 6:**
Students turn in their reports; discussion of higher-level thinking skills and the project in general.		
STUDENTS TURN IN WORK		
HOUR 7:	**HOUR 8:**	**HOUR 9:**

Lesson Plans and Notes

HOUR 1: Explain the project and distribute assignment sheets. It is suggested that only one of the projects be used with a particular group of students, since all four projects are so similar in structure. However, another option is to let each student choose from among the four project titles and pursue the subject of greatest interest. During this hour establish the due dates, first for notecards, bibliographies, and outlines, then for final written reports. A due date can also be set for rough drafts if that part of the writing process is to be emphasized. These projects are designed for students who are capable of independent learning (in other words, students who are advanced in skills development). The amount of independence allowed can be reduced by providing more classroom time for research and writing.

Note:

- There is a self-evaluation form provided at the end of the student material (following "Inventions and Discoveries") that can serve several purposes. It is often useful to hand it out during the first hour so students get a clear idea of the kinds of things being emphasized in this independent project. Here are some suggestions for using the self-evaluation form:
  a. Give the project a double grade, with your grade above a line and the student's below it.
  b. Keep the form (or a copy of it) for parent conferences. Interesting insights into a student's self-concept and sense of quality can be gleaned from a self-evaluation.
  c. Use the form for your own grading of each student and give point values for every category. This offers an excellent opportunity to make side-by-side comparisons with the student's evaluations.
  d. Give the project a grade that is an average between yours and the student's.
  e. Allow students to give themselves a final grade that is recorded.

HOUR 2: Students turn in their notecards, bibliographies, and outlines. Spend the hour discussing the students' progress and any research problems, discoveries, or questions they have.

Note:

- Be sure to carefully evaluate students' notecards and outlines *before* they begin to write reports. This is the critical stage where they learn to synthesize information into a smoothly presented report and *they need your help.*

HOUR 3: Notecards, bibliographies, and outlines are returned. The hour is spent going over common mistakes. Then have students begin writing while those with special problems or questions about their graded material meet with the teacher.

HOUR 4: Students turn in their completed research papers. For the rest of the hour hold a discussion about higher level thinking skills and how they were applied in this project. Why are they important to students who want to learn on their own? During the discussion briefly outline the levels of thinking skills:

Knowledge	Analysis
Comprehension	Synthesis
Application	Evaluation

Each of these levels is important in an independent project. Students are asked to think about how a project such as this prepares them for the future. Does higher education require independent learning skills? How about the occupations they are interested in? How is a person who can read, write, find information, plan projects, solve problems, discipline him or herself to work independently, to critically evaluate his or her own work, and to make a quality presentation to others equipped for a rapidly changing world? Students are encouraged to discuss the personal benefits of independent learning.

Note:

- The discussion during Hour 4 can also focus on the content of what students learned during their research. Each student should have something to contribute. This hour offers an excellent opportunity for a group discussion, which is an important form of presentation.

General Notes About This Project:

- Evaluation sheets for notecards and writing are provided in the Teacher's Introduction to the Student Research Guide (see Appendix). In addition, these projects offer excellent opportunities for requiring students to use the checklists and informational handouts that are supplied in the Student Research Guide. Perhaps most valuable will be the "Daily Log" in which students keep track of their progress, and the blank "Skills Chart" on which they record their skills development.

- As a follow-up to any of these projects, you may want to create another project that allows students to develop posters, murals, time-lines, or some other visual method of expressing what they have learned. Oral presentations to the class can be included.

THE FIFTY STATES OF AMERICA
Student Assignment Sheet

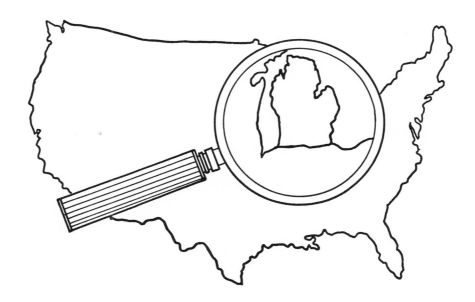

The United States of America is a large country with a central government that passes laws and speaks for the people of the entire nation. But within the country are 50 smaller governments that represent the people of individual states. Each state is a fascinating research topic, with its own history, geography, famous people, and interesting tales. In a time of rapid transportation and instant communication, it is important to learn about parts of the country other than your own state, to become familiar with where and how neighboring (or cross-country) Americans live.

This is a research/report project on the states of America. Choose one of the fifty states as your subject: the only requirement for your choice is that *it cannot be your home state* (so you really have 49 to choose from). Write a report about the state you've chosen; you may also be required to make an oral presentation to the class. Here is the assignment.

I. Choose a state from the list below. Remember, it cannot be your home state.

Alabama	Indiana	Nebraska	South Carolina
Alaska	Iowa	Nevada	South Dakota
Arizona	Kansas	New Hampshire	Tennessee
Arkansas	Kentucky	New Jersey	Texas
California	Louisiana	New Mexico	Utah
Colorado	Maine	New York	Vermont
Connecticut	Maryland	North Carolina	Virginia
Delaware	Massachusetts	North Dakota	Washington
Florida	Michigan	Ohio	West Virginia
Georgia	Minnesota	Oklahoma	Wisconsin
Hawaii	Mississippi	Oregon	Wyoming
Idaho	Missouri	Pennsylvania	
Illinois	Montana	Rhode Island	

THE STATE I HAVE CHOSEN TO STUDY IS: _____

II. Find at least five sources of information about the state.
   A. No more than two of these sources can be encyclopedias.
   B. Make a bibliography card for each source.

III. Find at least 25 facts about the state. Each fact should be neatly recorded on a notecard. You may use any facts you wish. Here are some suggestions:
   A. Capital city and other important cities
   B. Population: how many and what kinds of people
      1. Occupations
      2. Racial and ethnic groups
      3. Religions
      4. Population distribution
      5. Urban/rural dwellers
      6. Birth and death rates
   C. Wealth (taxes paid, average per capita income, amount spent on education and welfare, and so forth)
   D. Type of government and number of people in the state government
   E. Primary industries
   F. Interesting stories and folklore
   G. Important people outside of the state government
   H. Tourist areas
   I. Historical sites
   J. Important dates and events
   K. Natural resources
   L. Weather and climate
   M. Types of agriculture
   N. Major rivers, lakes, mountains, and other land forms
   O. State flower, bird, song, flag, nickname, slogan, and so forth

IV. Arrange your notecards in a logical order, then make an outline showing how the facts will be divided into paragraphs. Your notecards and outline will be handed in. Record the due date on the line below.

V. When the graded notecards and outline are returned, begin writing a report. A date will be set when your report is due. Record this date on the line below, and be sure to have the report completed on time.

VI. The report should be at least four pages long. Do your best writing, and follow your outline as closely as possible. Attach the graded outline to your report before handing it in.

VII. If you are to present your report to the class, be sure to use proper presentation skills. Make a poster or other visual display to go along with the oral report.

DUE DATES

Notecards, bibliography, and outline: _____

*Rough draft report: _____

Final report: _____

*You may not be required to turn in a rough draft.

FOREIGN COUNTRIES
Student Assignment Sheet

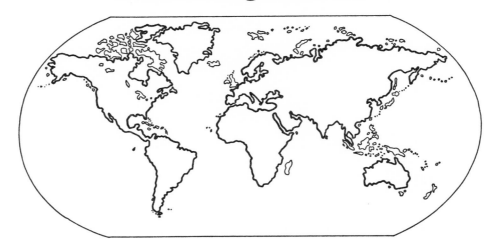

Ever since World War I the United States has been a world power with interests around the globe. Most people in the world know about the United States of America, but many Americans don't know very much about other countries or the people in them. This is unfortunate because America deals with these countries all the time. As we move into the twenty-first century Americans need to recognize the advantages of becoming acquainted with their global neighbors. Studying foreign countries in school is a first step toward better understanding and increased cooperation in the real world.

   This is a research/report project on foreign countries: choose a country other than the United States as a topic. You will write a report about the country you have chosen, and you may also be required to make an oral presentation to the class. Here is the assignment.

I.   Choose a country from the list below. If you want to study a country that is not in the list, have it approved by the teacher.

Afghanistan	Germany (East)	Netherlands
Angola	Germany (West)	Nicaragua
Argentina	Greece	Niger
Australia	Greenland	Northern Ireland
Austria	Haiti	Norway
Belgium	India	Pakistan
Bolivia	Ireland	Panama
Brazil	Israel	Paraguay
Bulgaria	Italy	Peru
Canada	Jamaica	Philippines
Chile	Japan	Poland
Congo	Jordan	Portugal
Cuba	Kenya	Romania
Czechoslovakia	Kuwait	Saudi Arabia
Denmark	Laos	South Africa
Ecuador	Lebanon	Soviet Union
Egypt	Libya	Spain
El Salvador	Mexico	Sweden
Finland	Morocco	Syria
France	Mozambique	Turkey

THE COUNTRY I HAVE CHOSEN TO STUDY IS: _____

II. Find at least five sources of information about the country you have chosen to study.
    A. No more than two of these sources can be encyclopedias.
    B. Make a bibliography card for each source.

III. Find at least 25 facts about the country. Each fact should be neatly recorded on a notecard. You may use any facts you wish. Here are some suggestions:
    A. Capital city and other important cities
    B. Population: how many and what kinds of people
       1. Occupations
       2. Racial and ethnic groups
       3. Population distribution
       4. Urban/rural dwellers
       5. Birth and death rates
    C. Wealth (per capita income, imports, exports, debt, amount of foreign aid, national budget)
    D. Primary industries and businesses
    E. Interesting stories and folklore
    F. Languages
    G. Religions
    H. Geographic location
    I. Type of government
    J. Leaders
    K. Important or famous people outside of government
    L. Tourist areas
    M. Historical events and dates of importance
    N. Natural resources
    O. Weather and climate
    P. Types of agriculture
    Q. Major rivers, lakes, mountains, and other landforms
    R. Festivals, traditions, customs
    S. Current events.

IV. Arrange your notecards in a logical order, then make an outline showing how the facts will be divided into paragraphs. Your notecards and outline will be handed in. Record the due date on the line below.

V. When the graded notecards and outline are returned, begin writing a report. A date will be set when your report is due. Record this date on the line below, and be sure to have the report completed on time.

VI. The report should be at least four pages long. Do your best writing, and follow your outline as closely as possible. Attach the graded outline to your report before handing it in.

VII. If you are to present your report to the class, be sure to use proper presentation skills. Make a poster or other visual display to go along with the oral report.

DUE DATES

Notecards, bibliography, and outline: _____

*Rough draft report: _____

Final report: _____

*You may not be required to turn in a rough draft.

Name _____ Date _____

THE WORLD OF SCIENCE
Student Assignment Sheet

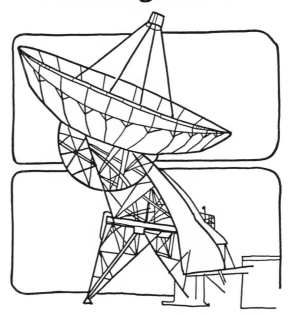

The world of science offers many fascinating, mysterious, and thought-provoking areas of study. Basically, science is the study of nature, in all its diverse forms. There is a branch of science for every aspect of nature, from the farthest reaches of the universe to the tiniest building blocks of atoms. Within this range there should be something of interest for you.

This is a research/report project on the world of science. Choose an area that interests you, and write a report about at least one specific topic. You may also be required to make an oral presentation to the class. Here is the assignment.

I. Choose an area of science from the list below. If you want to study an area that is not in the list, have it approved by the teacher.

Archaeology	Electronics	Medicine	Psychology
Astronomy	Entomology	Meteorology	Zoology
Biology	Geology	Oceanography	
Botany	Genetics	Paleontology	
Chemistry	Mathematics	Physics	

THE AREA OF SCIENCE I HAVE CHOSEN TO STUDY IS _____

II. Identify two or three specific research topics that relate to your chosen area of science before selecting one to write a report about. Study general reference books, like encyclopedias, to find topics that have plenty of information available. See point IV for topic suggestions.

MY TOPIC CHOICES ARE   1. _____

2. _____

3. _____

III. Find at least five sources of information about the topic you have chosen.
  A. No more than two of these sources can be encyclopedias.
  B. Make a bibliography card for each source.

IV. Find at least 25 facts about the topic you have chosen. Each fact should be neatly recorded on a notecard. You may use any facts you wish. Here are some suggestions that should help you choose a topic *and* decide what kinds of facts to search for:
  A. History: A time-line description of important events.
  B. Major discoveries: Who, what, where, when, how.
  C. Important people: What they accomplished and how their achievements contributed to science today; brief biographies.
  D. Fields of study: Every science is subdivided into fields of study. Choose one or two and explain what they are.
  E. Theories: Many times scientific ideas cannot be absolutely *proven,* so scientists develop theories, like the atomic structure theory (in chemistry) or theories about why the dinosaurs died (in paleontology) or theories of evolution (in biology). Explain a theory that has been developed within your science area.
  F. Special topic: You may have a special or favorite topic, such as computers (in electronics), plant hybrids (in genetics), whales (in zoology), anorexia nervosa (in psychology), or ant colonies (in entomology). Provide some information about your special topic to show why you are interested in it.
  G. General description: Explain generally what the area of science is concerned with. What does an astronomer do? What is geology? What kinds of things would you study in a physics class?
  H. Careers: What kinds of career possibilities are available within the science area? What jobs could you have if you were a meteorologist? What job opportunities are there in medicine? What can a mathematician do for a career?

Put an asterisk next to the one you finally choose to do a report on.

  V. Arrange your notecards in a logical order, then make an outline showing how the facts will be divided into paragraphs. Your notecards and outline will be handed in. Record the due date on the line below.

  VI. When the graded notecards and outline are returned, begin writing a report. A date will be set when your report is due. Record this date on the line below, and be sure to have the report completed on time.

  VII. The report should be at least four pages long. Do your best writing, and follow your outline as closely as possible. Attach the graded outline to your report before handing it in.

  VIII. If you are to present your report to the class, be sure to use proper presentation skills. Make a poster or other visual display to go along with the oral report.

DUE DATES

Notecards, bibliography, and outline: _____

*Rough draft report: _____

Final report: _____

*You may not be required to turn in a rough draft.

Name _____ Date _____

INVENTIONS AND DISCOVERIES
Student Assignment Sheet

Human beings are creative creatures. In a matter of a few thousand years we have gone from the invention of the wheel to the development of the computer, with countless inventions and discoveries in between. It is the impulse to develop new things, to explore unknown areas, and to think of ways to make life easier that has brought us to the computer age. The time-line of human inventiveness is fascinating, and it is filled with interesting things to study. The difficulty with such a study lies not in deciding what general area to investigate, but in narrowing the vast field down to a single topic.

This is a research/report project on inventions and discoveries. Choose an invention or discovery as your subject, and then find information about it and the person or persons responsible for creating and discovering it. Write a report about the invention or discovery you have chosen; you may also be required to make an oral presentation to the class. Here is the assignment.

I. Choose an invention or discovery to study. The list below is provided to help you, but there are *thousands* of inventions that could be studied. If you want to study something that is not in the list, have it approved by the teacher.

Airplane	Jet plane	Rifle
Assembly line	Klieg light	Rocketry
Automobile	Light bulb	Saxophone
Battery	Microchip	Steam engine
Camera	Microscope	Steel
CAT scan	Morse code	Telegraph
Computer	Nitrogen	Telephone
Cotton gin	Pluto	Television
Diesel engine	Peanut butter	Transistor
Electricity	Periodic law	Ultraviolet light
Fahrenheit scale	Phonograph	Uranium 235
Genes	Prairie schooner	V-eight engine
Geometry	Quasar	Violin
Gravity	Radar	Windmill
Gyroscope	Radio	X-ray
Holography	Refrigerator	Zeppelin

THE INVENTION OR DISCOVERY I HAVE CHOSEN TO STUDY IS _____

_____

II. Find at least five sources of information about the invention or discovery you have chosen to study.

    A. No more than two of these sources can be encyclopedias.

    B. Make a bibliography card for each source.

III. Find at least 25 facts about the invention or discovery and about the people most responsible for creating or identifying it. Each fact should be neatly recorded on a notecard. You may use any facts you wish. Here are some suggestions:

    A. Important people: brief biographies

    B. Important dates: a time line

    C. Related inventions and discoveries

    D. Uses for the invention or discovery

    E. Explanation of how the invention works

    F. Explanation of why the discovery was important

    G. Explanation of how the invention or discovery is being used today

    H. Description of additional or new things that the invention or discovery has made possible in today's world

    I. Explanation of why anyone thought the invention or discovery was worth pursuing: *why* was it invented or discovered?

    J. Materials, special parts, or new research that were necessary to create the invention or make the discovery

IV. Arrange your notecards in a logical order, then make an outline showing how the facts will be divided into paragraphs. Your notecards and outline will be handed in. Record the due date on the line below.

V. When the graded notecards and outline are returned, begin writing a report. A date will be set when your report is due. Record this date on the line below, and be sure to have the report completed on time.

VI. The report should be at least four pages long. Do your best writing, and follow the outline as closely as possible. Attach the graded outline to your report before handing it in.

VII. If you are to present your report to the class, be sure to use proper presentation skills. Make a poster or other visual display to go along with the oral report.

DUE DATES

Notecards, bibliography, and outline: _____

*Rough draft report: _____

Final report: _____

*You may not be required to turn in a rough draft.

Name _____ Date _____

STUDENT SELF-EVALUATION FORM

The most valuable evaluation of an independent project is your own. Rate yourself in each category below. This should be an honest appraisal of your work, based upon the experience of a person who really knows—you.

EVALUATE YOURSELF IN THE FOLLOWING AREAS:

I. Following the outline
    A. Topic selection
        1. Did you choose an interesting topic?   _____ (0-5 pts.)

        2. Did you choose a challenging topic?   _____ (0-5 pts.)

        3. Did you choose a topic that had plenty of information available? _____ (0-5 pts.)

                                              Subtotal (15 possible) _____
    B. Sources of information
        1. Evaluate the quality of the sources you used.   _____ (0-5 pts.)

        2. Give yourself from 0-10 points, depending on how much effort
           was put into finding information.   _____ (0-10 pts.)

        3. Evaluate your bibliography cards for accuracy and
           completeness.   _____ (0-5 pts.)

        4. Evaluate your bibliography cards for neatness.   _____ (0-5 pts.)

                                              Subtotal (25 possible) _____
    C. Facts and notecards
        1. Evaluate the quality and usefulness of facts you recorded.   _____ (0-5 pts.)

        2. Give yourself from 0–10 points, depending on how much
           effort was put into recording facts.   _____ (0-10 pts.)

        3. Evaluate your notecards for accuracy and completeness.   _____ (0-5 pts.)

        4. Evaluate your notecards for neatness.   _____ (0-5 pts.)

                                              Subtotal (25 possible) _____
    D. Outline
        1. Evaluate the quality and usefulness of your outline.   _____ (0-5 pts.)

        2. Give yourself from 0-10 points, depending on how much
           effort was put into producing an outline.   _____ (0-10 pts.)

        3. Evaluate your outline for accuracy and completeness.   _____ (0-5 pts.)

        4. Evaluate your outline for neatness.   _____ (0-5 pts.)

                                              Subtotal (25 possible) _____
    E. Report
        1. Evaluate how well your report is organized.   _____ (0-5 pts.)

        2. Evaluate how clearly you explained or presented information.   _____ (0-5 pts.)

3. Give yourself from 0-10 points, depending on how much effort was put into your report. _____ (0-10 pts.)

4. Evaluate how well you understand the information that is recorded in your report. _____ (0-5 pts.)

5. Evaluate your report for accuracy and completeness. _____ (0-5 pts.)

6. Evaluate your report for neatness. _____ (0-5 pts.)

7. Give yourself 15 points if you handed in your report on or before the due date. Give yourself 0 points if you didn't. _____ (0-15 pts.)

Subtotal (50 possible) _____

II. Writing skills

A. Construction and organization
1. Does the report have an appropriate title? _____ (0-5 pts.)

2. Do the paragraphs closely follow the outline? _____ (0-5 pts.)

3. Does each paragraph have a main idea? _____ (0-5 pts.)

4. Is the report introduced in an interesting manner? _____ (0-5 pts.)

5. Does the report have a good conclusion? _____ (0-5 pts.)

6. Give yourself from 0-5 points, depending on how much effort was put into the construction and organization of the report. _____ (0-5 pts.)

Subtotal (30 possible) _____

B. Grammar and basic English
1. Are all sentences complete? (Does each have a subject and a predicate [verb]?) _____ (0-5 pts.)

2. Is punctuation used correctly throughout? _____ (0-5 pts.)

3. Are all beginnings of sentences and proper nouns capitalized? _____ (0-5 pts.)

4. Are all words spelled correctly? _____ (0-5 pts.)

5. Are all words used correctly? (Do you know all the words you used?) _____ (0-5 pts.)

6. Give yourself from 0-5 points, depending on how much effort was put into using correct grammar and proper basic English. _____ (0-5 pts.)

Subtotal (30 possible) _____

FINAL TOTAL (200 possible) _____

III. Circle the grade below that you believe is a fair assessment of the work you did on this project. Take into account both effort and quality. Obviously, this grade will depend upon your definition of *effort* and *quality*.

A+   A   A−   B+   B   B−   C+   C   C−   D+   D   D−   F

IV. Record your comments about the project on the back of this page.

YEAR IN REVIEW

Teacher Preview

General Explanation:
This is a culminating, or year-end, project in which students write a newsletter (or "magazine") to their parents telling them about the school year. In their newsletter, students describe activities, projects, and events that have stood out as highlights of the year. There is no handout included with the project. The project's basic structure is provided as a starting point, since there are innumerable variations that can be tried.

Length of Project: 4 hours

Level of Independence: Advanced

Goals:

1. To encourage students to inform their parents about the school they attend and the activities in which they participate.

2. To promote writing as a means of communication.

3. To emphasize independent writing.

During This Project Students Will:

1. Choose events from the school year to report on.

2. Assemble material for newsletter articles.

3. Write articles about their school.

4. Design a newsletter.

Skills:

Collecting data	Identifying problems
Interviewing	Persistence
Listening	Setting personal goals
Summarizing	Self-confidence
Grammar	Handwriting
Neatness	Accepting responsibility
Paragraphs	Concentration
Sentences	Controlling behavior
Spelling	Individualized study habits
Group planning	Time management

Organizing	Working with others
Outlining	Personal motivation
Setting objectives	Self-awareness
Selecting topics	Sense of "quality"
Divergent-convergent-	Creative expression
evaluative thinking	Writing
Meeting deadlines	Following and changing plans

Handouts Provided:

- No handouts are needed for this project.

PROJECT CALENDAR:

HOUR 1: _____ The project is introduced, categories or sections for the newsletter are identified, and each student selects a topic about which to write an article.	**HOUR 2:** _____ Students bring written articles to class and meet in small groups to develop individual sections of the newsletter.	**HOUR 3:** _____ Each section of the newspaper is completed and handed in. STUDENTS TURN IN WORK
HOUR 4: _____ Newsletters are collated, stapled, and distributed (or mailed). Articles must be duplicated before the hour begins. PREPARATION REQUIRED	**HOUR 5:** _____	**HOUR 6:** _____
HOUR 7: _____	**HOUR 8:** _____	**HOUR 9:** _____

Lesson Plans and Notes

HOUR 1: In class discuss the idea of a newsletter for parents. Focus the discussion on what categories, or sections, the newsletter should include, and have the students produce a list of specific topics under each category. Assign a topic to each student (by choice, lottery, or random assignment) and set a due date for finished articles to be brought to class.

Notes:

- To avoid having the newsletter become too large to be practical, place a maximum length of one handwritten page on each article. This limit may even be reduced to one-half page.
- Here are some suggested categories for sections of a "Year in Review" newsletter. These may not apply in certain situations, and there will undoubtedly be additional ones suggested by the students. Possible categories are:
  a. Field trips
  b. Interviews/personalities
  c. Courses and projects
  d. Special activities and programs
  e. Anecdotes and stories
  f. Athletics
  g. Cartoons
  h. Editorials
  i. Current events
  j. Special awards and achievements
  k. Extracurricular activities
  l. Fads and fashions
- During this hour also decide on a title for the newsletter.

HOUR 2: Students bring their articles to class. Organize the students into small groups to prepare each section of the newsletter. For example, all students who wrote articles about field trips are in one group, those who conducted interviews and wrote personality sketches are in another, and so forth. There is no specific number of students in each group. One group may have only two members, and another might have eight. Each group designs one section for the newsletter, which consists of the articles its members have written, a "catchy" title, an introductory paragraph, a list of contributing authors, and perhaps some artwork.

HOUR 3: Small groups meet and continue working on the newsletter. Completed sections are turned in at the end of the hour. Choose one or two students to work on a cover page for the newsletter.

Notes:

- After proofreading each section, have the newsletter reproduced, in whatever quantity is needed, before Hour 4 begins.
- It may be necessary to add an hour if material needs to be rewritten. If this is the case, earmark Hour 4 for discussion of mistakes and for rewriting, and add a fifth hour for putting the newsletter together.

HOUR 4: Newsletters are collated, stapled, distributed, or addressed for mailing. This is the end of the project and a good way to culminate the year: students make use of their skills for independent learning, and parents are informed about the events of the school year.

Appendix

Teacher's Introduction to the Student Research Guide

Many of the projects in *Learning on Your Own!* require students to conduct research. Few children, however, possess the necessary skills to successfully complete this type of project. The research guide is designed to help them learn and practice some basic skills: how to locate, record, organize, and present information about topics they study. Even though the handouts in the guide are detailed, students will need some guidance and instructional support from you as they undertake their first research projects.

This Teacher's Introduction to the guide contains four forms that can be used to evaluate how well students do on (1) writing, (2) notecards, (3) posters, and (4) oral presentations. These are designed as optional evaluations that may be used with many projects in the book, regardless of subject or topic area.

Teaching a lesson on "how to use the library" is one type of instructional support you should give students to prepare them for research. Therefore, a "Typical Library Quiz" is also included in this Teacher's Introduction for you to give students after they have become acquainted with the library.

The Student Research Guide will be most useful to students if you spend some time explaining the following topics to your class.

1. *Library skills:* Use an example of a real library to explain how books and periodicals are categorized and where they are stored. Whatever library is most likely to be used by students should serve as a model. Cover these things in a library skills unit:

    a. The card catalog (handout provided)

    b. How to find a book from its call number (handout provided)

    c. The *Reader's Guide to Periodical Literature* and other periodical guides (handout provided)

    d. How to ask questions and use librarians as helpful resources

    e. Other kinds of information and services offered by libraries

2. *Notecards and bibliographies:* Provide a variety of examples of properly made notecards and bibliographies for students to use as models. (Reference handout provided.) Explain how to use a numbering system to cross-reference a set of notecards with a bibliography. Spend enough time on bibliographies to ensure

that students know how to write them for the most common sources (books, magazines, encyclopedias, and newspapers).

3. *The* **Readers' Guide to Periodical Literature**: You can teach students how to use this valuable resource before they ever go to a library. Contact the librarian and ask for old monthly *RGPL* discards. Collect them until you have at least one for every student in the room. During your library skills unit pass the guides out and write ten topics on the board, for example:

   a. The president of the United States
   b. The automobile industry
   c. Basketball (or football, baseball, hockey, and so on)
   d. Ballet
   e. Acid rain
   f. Poland
   g. Israel
   h. Martin Luther King, Jr.
   i. Satellites
   j. Agriculture

   Tell students to choose five topics, find at least one article about each and properly record the title of the article, the author of the article, the name of the magazine, its volume number, the pages on which it can be found, and the date it was published.

4. *Common sources of information:* Encourage students to make extensive use of encyclopedias, magazines such as *National Geographic, Junior Scholastic, Newsweek* and others that are readily available, textbooks and workbooks, materials from home, and whatever other sources are in the classroom or school library. Always require that adequate information from these common sources be available before allowing a research project to begin.

The Student Research Guide is primarily a series of handouts. You may want to give them to students as a complete booklet or hand them out individually to be used with separate, specific research lessons. The research guide is supplied as an aid to help students tackle projects that require research and independent work. The handouts *supplement* what is being taught in the projects, and they provide excellent reference materials for independent learning.

Name _____ Date _____

WRITING EVALUATION

Paper or Report Title: _____

Your written paper (or report) has been evaluated for basics such as grammar, spelling, punctuation, capitalization, vocabulary, sentence structure, paragraph formation, and idea development. This is a report on your ability to use these basic skills to produce correct, interesting, and informative written material.

I. Correct use of the parts of speech

    A. Nouns   2 pts. _____

    B. Pronouns   2 pts. _____

    C. Verbs   2 pts. _____

    D. Adjectives   2 pts. _____

    E. Adverbs   2 pts. _____

    F. Prepositions   2 pts. _____

    G. Conjunctions   2 pts. _____

    H. Interjections   2 pts. _____

                            Subtotal (16 points possible) _____

    Notes: _____

_____

_____

II. Accurate spelling

    A. Correct spelling of unfamiliar words: Points are deducted for not using a dictionary to look up unfamiliar words.   5 pts. _____

    B. Correct spelling of common words: Points are deducted for careless mistakes.   5 pts. _____

                             Subtotal (10 points possible) _____

    Notes: _____

_____

_____

III. Correct use of punctuation and capitalization

    A. Periods   2 pts. _____

    B. Question marks   2 pts. _____

C. Exclamation points   2 pts. _____

D. Commas   2 pts. _____

E. Apostrophes   2 pts. _____

F. Brackets, parentheses, quotation marks   2 pts. _____

G. Colons, semicolons, dashes   2 pts. _____

H. First word of every sentence capitalized   2 pts. _____

I. Proper nouns capitalized   2 pts. _____

J. Words capitalized that are not supposed to be (Points are deducted for this.)   2 pts. _____

Subtotal (20 points possible) _____

Notes: _____

_____

_____

IV. Proper use of words (vocabulary)

A. Unusual or uncommon words are used in context (the student understands the
definitions and correct use of words included in the paper).   3 pts. _____

B. Correct use of common words like there, their, they're; to, too, two; no, any.   3 pts. _____

C. Explanation of words the reader may not understand.   3 pts. _____

D. Effective use of descriptive words.   3 pts. _____

Subtotal (12 points possible) _____

Notes: _____

_____

_____

V. Proper sentence structure

A. Complete sentences: Each sentence has a subject and a predicate (verb).   5 pts. _____

B. Run-on sentences: Points are deducted for using poorly punctuated, run-on
sentences.   5 pts. _____

C. Sentences are clearly stated, not wordy or confusing.   5 pts. _____

Subtotal (15 points possible) _____

Notes: _____

_____

_____

VI. Organized paragraphs

    A. Each paragraph has one main idea.   3 pts. _____

    B. Each paragraph has a topic sentence.   3 pts. _____

    C. Each paragraph has a concluding sentence.   3 pts. _____

    D. Paragraphs follow one another smoothly; they provide continuity.   3 pts. _____

    E. The paper (or report) has good introductory and concluding paragraphs.   3 pts. _____

Subtotal (15 points possible) _____

Notes: _____

_____

_____

VII. Idea development

    A. The report is interesting and shows effort and creativity.   12 pts. _____

Notes: _____

_____

_____

TOTAL (100 points possible) _____

Additional Comments: _____

_____

_____

_____

_____

_____

Name _____ Date _____

NOTECARD EVALUATION

Below are ten areas for which your notecards have been evaluated. This breakdown of your final score, which is at the bottom of the sheet, indicates the areas where improvement is needed and where you have done well.

	EXCELLENT (10 pts.)	VERY GOOD (9 pts.)	GOOD (7 pts.)	FAIR (6 pts.)	POOR (4 pts.)	NOT DONE OR INCOMPLETE (0 pts.)
1. Bibliography	_____	_____	_____	_____	_____	_____
2. Reference between notecards and bibliography	_____	_____	_____	_____	_____	_____
3. Headings and subheadings	_____	_____	_____	_____	_____	_____
4. Organizing information onto cards so it can be understood and used later without confusion: numbering system	_____	_____	_____	_____	_____	_____
5. Neatness (If reading or use of the cards is made difficult because of sloppy writing,"POOR" will be checked.)	_____	_____	_____	_____	_____	_____
6. Recording meaningful information (Everything recorded on notecards should relate directly to your topic.)	_____	_____	_____	_____	_____	_____
7. Spelling	_____	_____	_____	_____	_____	_____
8. Accuracy of information	_____	_____	_____	_____	_____	_____
9. Quantity (Did you do as much work as you were supposed to, or should have, to complete the project?)	_____	_____	_____	_____	_____	_____
10. Information properly recorded (Facts must be brief and understandable. It is best to condense information into concise statements. Entire paragraphs should not be copied onto notecards. Direct quotes must be identified.)	_____	_____	_____	_____	_____	_____

FINAL SCORE _____ (100 possible)

COMMENTS _____

_____

_____

Name _____ Date _____

POSTER EVALUATION

Below are ten areas for which your poster has been evaluated. This breakdown of your final score, which is at the bottom of the sheet, indicates the areas where improvement is needed and where you have done well.

	EXCELLENT (10 pts.)	VERY GOOD (9 pts.)	GOOD (7 pts.)	FAIR (6 pts.)	POOR (4 pts.)	NOT DONE OR INCOMPLETE (0 pts.)
1. Facts which your poster teaches (at least twenty)	____	____	____	____	____	____
2. Poster "goes along with" your written report	____	____	____	____	____	____
3. Visual impact: use of color, headings, and lettering	____	____	____	____	____	____
4. Drawings (at least one)	____	____	____	____	____	____
5. Pictures, articles, headlines, quotes, charts, graphs, diagrams, explanations, and so forth	____	____	____	____	____	____
6. Organization of material	____	____	____	____	____	____
7. Neatness	____	____	____	____	____	____
8. Spelling, grammar, writing skills	____	____	____	____	____	____
9. Accurate information	____	____	____	____	____	____
10. Specific topic; proper material (Did you do a good job of presenting your topic?)	____	____	____	____	____	____

FINAL SCORE _____ (100 possible)

COMMENTS _____

_____

_____

Name _____ Date _____

ORAL PRESENTATION EVALUATION

This form shows how your oral presentation has been evaluated. It indicates areas where improvement is needed and where you have done well.

Topic _____

I. Presentation (50 points possible)

   A. Eye contact.   3 pts. _____
   B. Voice projection.   3 pts. _____
   C. Use of the English language.   3 pts. _____
   D. Inflection.   3 pts. _____
   E. Articulation.   3 pts. _____
   F. Posture.   3 pts. _____
   G. Use of hands.   3 pts. _____
   H. Appropriate vocabulary.   3 pts. _____
   I. Accurate information.   10 pts. _____
   J. Information is easy to understand.   3 pts. _____
   K. Enough information.   3 pts. _____
   L. Information relates to topic.   3 pts. _____
   M. Effort.   7 pts. _____

                                                 Subtotal _____

II. Visual or Extra Materials (30 points possible)

   A. Information is easy to understand.   3 pts. _____
   B. Information relates to the oral report.   3 pts. _____
   C. Information is current.   3 pts. _____
   D. Information is accurate.   3 pts. _____
   E. Enough information.   3 pts. _____
   F. Neatness.   3 pts. _____
   G. Spelling.   3 pts. _____
   H. Artistic effort.   3 pts. _____
   I. Research effort.   3 pts. _____
   J Appropriate vocabulary.   3 pts. _____

                                                 Subtotal _____

III. Question-Answer Period (20 points possible)

   A. Confidence in knowledge of topic.   3 pts. _____
   B. Ability to answer reasonable questions.   3 pts. _____
   C. Answers are accurate.   3 pts. _____
   D. Student is willing to admit limits of knowledge or understanding such as "I don't know."   2 pts. _____
   E. Answers are brief.   3 pts. _____
   F. Student exhibits ability to infer or hypothesize an answer from available information.   3 pts. _____
   G. Student appears to have put effort into learning about this topic.   3 pts. _____

                                                 Subtotal _____

                         TOTAL (100 pts. possible) _____

COMMENTS _____

_____

Name _____ Date _____

TYPICAL LIBRARY QUIZ

How well do you know the library? Answer these questions and find out.

1. List four kinds of information you can find on a card in the card catalog:

    a. _____

    b. _____

    c. _____

    d. _____

2. What does "jB" tell you about a book when it precedes the call number?

    _____

3. What does "jR" tell you about a book when it precedes the call number?

    _____

4. Suppose you are writing a report about polar bears. You look up "polar bears" in the card catalog but find only a few sources. What would you look under next?

    _____

5. If you are looking for a book with the call number j598.132/D43, would you find it before or after j598.2/D42?

    _____

6. If you are looking for "G-men" in the card catalog, you may find a card that says "G-men, see U.S. Federal Bureau of Investigation." Where would you look next?

    _____

7. List these call numbers in the order that they would be found on the shelf:

    j973.15   j973.35   j973.3   j973
    Ad32   Ab24   Cy31   Ad55

    a. _____   c. _____

    b. _____   d. _____

8. Books of fiction are shelved alphabetically by _____.

9. Biographies are shelved alphabetically by _____ — _____ .

10. What do the words or letters on the front of a card catalog drawer tell you? (example: Istanbul—jets)

   _____

11. How long can books be checked out of the library?

   _____

12. If the book you are looking for is not on the shelf, what should you do?

   _____

13. Where would you go to find a listing of all the magazines your library subscribes to? (Circle the correct answer.)

   a. Card catalog   d. Young adults

   b. History and travel   e. *Readers' Guide to Periodical Literature*

   c. Information desk

14. For *current* information, where should you check first?

   a. Encyclopedia   c. Card catalog

   b. *Readers' Guide to*   d. Book shelves
      Periodical Literature   e. Reference shelves

15. Below is an excerpt from the *Readers' Guide to Periodical Literature*. Look it over and then answer the questions:

   The real cost of a car. S. Porter, il Ladies Home J. 99:58 Je '82

   a. What is the title of the article? _____

   b. Who wrote the article? _____

   c. What month and year was the article published? _____

   d. What magazine published the article? _____

   e. In what volume of the magazine was the article published? _____

   f. On what page can the article be found? _____

   g. Where in the library would you be most likely to find this article?

   _____

Student Research Guide

STUDENT RESEARCH GUIDE

Research is the process you go through to find information about a topic that interests you. This guide explains some basic tools needed to find and record information. It gives advice about how to conduct a research project and also provides many suggestions for developing a *presentation* of the topic.

A list of skills that you will use during research projects includes finding resources, choosing topics, writing and notetaking, summarizing, organizing ideas, scanning, planning, and interpreting data. This guide will help in many of these areas.

Of course, the real quality of a project is determined by the personal characteristics you bring to it—things like patience, motivation, accuracy, neatness, humor, persistence, and creativity. There are no handouts in the Student Research Guide that teach these things, but they are perhaps the most essential ingredients of a successful project.

Your Research Guide contains the following handouts:

"Outlining"
"Bibliographies"
"Notecards and Bibliographies"
"Sending for Information"
"The Dewey Decimal Classification System"
"The Card Catalog"
"The Readers' Guide to Periodical Literature"
"Choosing a Subject"
"Audio-Visual and Written Information Guides"

"Where to Go or Write for Information"
"Project Fact Sheet"
"Project Fact Sheet: Example"
"Poster Display Sheet"
"Things to Check Before Giving Your Presentation"
"Visual Aids for the Oral Presentation"
"Things to Remember When Presenting Your Project"
"Daily Log"
"Blank Skills Chart"

OUTLINING

I. Outlining is like classification: it sorts ideas and facts into categories or like-groups. This is an important skill to have when you are conducting a research project because you must organize information before you can use it.

II. Outlining separates main ideas from details in two ways:

A. By symbols
   1. Alternating letters and numbers
   2. Same symbol = same importance

B. By indentation
   1. Indent more with each subheading
   2. Same margin = same importance

I.

II.

    A.

    B.

       1.

       2.

          a)

          b)

             (1)

             (2)

OUTLINING (continued)

III. It is very important to understand that every item in an outline can be expanded with additional research or new information. The outline below is incomplete, but it shows how to use symbols and indentation to organize facts and ideas into a logical order. When you make an outline, leave plenty of room between lines so additional ideas can be included later. Think of ways to expand this outline:

EXAMPLE: My Autobiography

I. Early years

  A. Birth

    1. Place

    2. Date

    3. Time

    4. Other details

  B. Family

    1. Father

    2. Mother

    3. Brothers and sisters

    4. Other members of the extended family

    5. Other important adults in your life

  C. First home

    1. Location and description

      a) address

      b) type of house

      c) color

      d) trees in yard

        (1) tall maple in back

        (2) two cherries in front

        (3) giant oak in side yard

          (a) rope swing

          (b) tree house

          (c) shade

            i. summer afternoon naps

            ii. lemonade stand three summers ago

    2. Neighborhood

    3. Experiences

II. School years

  A. School or schools attended

    1. School name and description

    2. Favorite teacher(s)

    3. Favorite subject(s)

  B. Significant experiences

    1. Vacations

    2. Births

    3. Deaths

    4. Adventures

    5. Ideas and beliefs

  C. Friends

III. Present

  A. Residence

  B. Family

  C. School

  D. Hobbies and interests

  E. Friends

IV. Future

  A. Education

  B. Career

  C. Personal goals

  D. Vacations—trips

  E. Family

BIBLIOGRAPHIES

A bibliography is a standard method for recording where information came from. It is important to be able to prove that research came from legitimate sources. Use the following forms when recording information for bibliographies:

I. When working with a book:

    A. Author's last name first
    B. Full title underlined
    C. Place of publication
    D. Date of publication
    E. Publisher
    F. Page(s)

NOTECARD FORM:

Galbraith, John K.
The Affluent Society
Boston
1966
Houghton Mifflin
76

STANDARD FORM:

    Galbraith, John K., The Affluent Society. Boston: Houghton Mifflin, 1966; 76.

II. When working with a periodical:

    A. Author's last name first
    B. Full article title in quotes
    C. Name of periodical underlined
    D. Volume number
    E. Date in parentheses
    F. Page(s)

NOTECARD FORM:

Lippman, Walter
"Cuba and the Nuclear Race"
Atlantic
211
(Feb. 1963)
55–58

STANDARD FORM:

    Lippman, Walter. "Cuba and the Nuclear Race." Atlantic 211 (February 1963): 55–58.

III. When working with newspaper articles:

    A. Author's last name first
    B. Full article title in quotes

    C. Name of paper underlined
    D. Date
    E. Section (some papers are not divided into sections)
    F. Page

NOTECARD FORM:

May, Clifford D.
"Campus Report: Computers In, Typewriters Out"
The New York Times
May 12, 1986

28

STANDARD FORM:

    May, Clifford D. "Campus Report: Computers In, Typewriters Out," The New York Times, May 12, 1986, p. 28.

IV. When working with an encyclopedia:

    A. Author's last name first
    B. Full title of article in quotes
    C. Name of encyclopedia underlined
    D. Date of publication in parentheses
    E. Volume number
    F. Page(s)

NOTECARD FORM:

Clutz, Donald G.
"Television"
Encyclopaedia Britannica
(1963)
21
910

STANDARD FORM:

    Clutz, Donald G. "Television," Encyclopaedia Britannica (1963), 21, 910.

NOTECARDS AND BIBLIOGRAPHIES

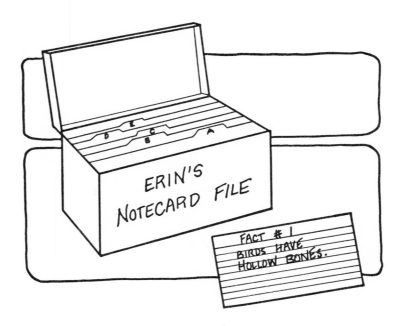

Notecards are used to record and collect information. Bibliography cards are used to tell where the information came from. Once information is gathered about a topic, notecards become the main tool for writing a report. Since each notecard contains a separate idea, you can arrange and rearrange these ideas into an order that becomes an outline for your report. If more information is needed about a particular fact, or, if something needs to be clarified, bibliography cards will tell which source to go to.

Each card should be numbered. It is *very* important that each notecard have a bibliography card number to tell where each fact came from. For example, if you study a unit called "Ecology" in science class, you could do a project about air pollution. Suppose you found information about air pollution in a book titled *Environmental Pollution*—you would make one bibliography card for this source, regardless of how many facts you obtained from it. If this book was the fifth source you used, the bibliography card for it would be numbered "5" in the upper right.

Now, suppose that the chapter on air pollution has four facts, or pieces of information, that you want to use. Make four notecards, each with a unit or course title at the top ("Ecology") and the topic being studied on the next line ("air pollution"). Number these cards in the upper right-hand corner, continuing the numbers from the last card of your fourth source. In other words, if you have 17 notecards from your first four sources, the next card you make will be number 18.

Next, tell where you found the information on each notecard. Do this by writing "bibliography card #5" at the bottom right of each of these four notecards. This clearly shows that you have to look at bibliography card number five to find out where the information came from.

Remember to put only one important fact on each notecard. Don't copy long passages from sources onto notecards; condense information into easily stated facts. If a quote is included in your report, however, it *should* be recorded word for word. Also, if you record your bibliography on notebook paper instead of notecards, each source must still be numbered.

Here is a sample notecard:

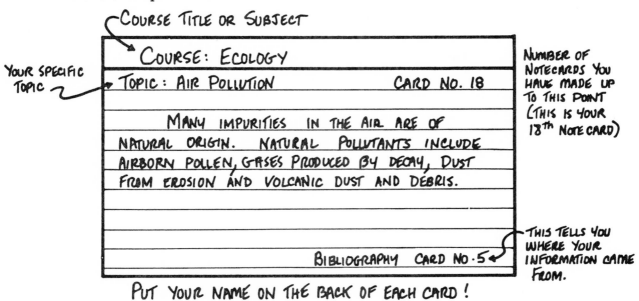

COURSE TITLE OR SUBJECT

YOUR SPECIFIC TOPIC

COURSE: ECOLOGY

TOPIC: AIR POLLUTION   CARD NO. 18

MANY IMPURITIES IN THE AIR ARE OF NATURAL ORIGIN. NATURAL POLLUTANTS INCLUDE AIRBORN POLLEN, GASES PRODUCED BY DECAY, DUST FROM EROSION AND VOLCANIC DUST AND DEBRIS.

BIBLIOGRAPHY CARD NO. 5

NUMBER OF NOTECARDS YOU HAVE MADE UP TO THIS POINT (THIS IS YOUR 18TH NOTE CARD)

THIS TELLS YOU WHERE YOUR INFORMATION CAME FROM.

PUT YOUR NAME ON THE BACK OF EACH CARD!

If you are required to record your bibliography on notecards, here is a sample bibliography card:

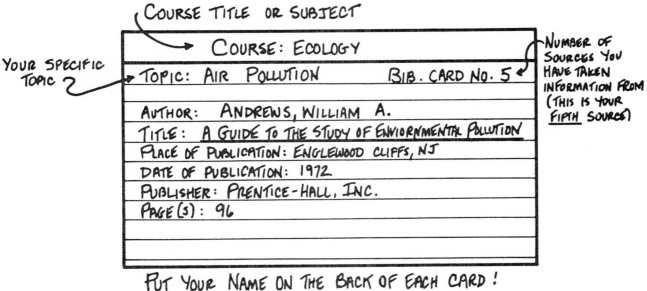

COURSE TITLE OR SUBJECT

YOUR SPECIFIC TOPIC

COURSE: ECOLOGY

TOPIC: AIR POLLUTION   BIB. CARD NO. 5

AUTHOR: ANDREWS, WILLIAM A.
TITLE: A GUIDE TO THE STUDY OF ENVIORNMENTAL POLLUTION
PLACE OF PUBLICATION: ENGLEWOOD CLIFFS, NJ
DATE OF PUBLICATION: 1972
PUBLISHER: PRENTICE-HALL, INC.
PAGE(S): 96

NUMBER OF SOURCES YOU HAVE TAKEN INFORMATION FROM (THIS IS YOUR FIFTH SOURCE)

PUT YOUR NAME ON THE BACK OF EACH CARD!

SENDING FOR INFORMATION

There are times when sending a letter is the best way to obtain information about a research topic. Unfortunately, many people write letters hastily. They don't take time to explain themselves clearly or else they come across sounding unprofessional and insincere. You should learn how to write a good letter so that, when confronted with a difficult project, you can get help from others. Study the outline below. It explains why letter writing is a useful research skill and what components should be included in the letters you write. Examples of two letter styles are provided.

I. Reasons for sending a letter:

    A. To obtain up-to-date information.

    B. To make contact with experts or specific organizations.

    C. To get specialized or technical information

    D. To ask for opinions and advice.

    E. To ask for suggestions of other places to look for information about the topic.

    F. To ask for free materials.

    G. To send special questions to authorities in the field you are studying.

II. Parts of a letter

A. Heading:	*Your* return address at the top of the letter, and the date right below your address.
B. Inside address:	The address of the person or organization to whom you are sending the letter.
C. Salutation:	Begin your letter with a salutation to the person you are sending it to: Dear Mr. Wilson; Dear Miss Goode; Dear Mrs. Smith; Dear Ms. Jones; Dear Sir.
D. Body:	Introduce yourself, explain your project, and ask for whatever assistance you are seeking. Be concise and clear in your writing; don't make someone guess what you want.
E. Complimentary close:	Show your respect by thanking the person to whom you have sent your letter for whatever help he or she can provide. Your letter might end like this:

"…I appreciate any advice or information you can offer to help me with my project.
Thank you."

Sincerely,

John Jones

F. Signature	Sign your name at the bottom of the letter, beneath the complimentary close.

EXAMPLE OF THE "BLOCK LETTER" STYLE

John Jones
1532 Hill Street
Bridgeton, TX 75588

March 16, 19XX

Dr. David Adamson
Entomological Society
113 Geneva Road
Fair Ridge, OH 45289

Dear Dr. Adamson:

I am an eighth-grade student at Bridgeton Middle School, and we are doing a science project on insects. I am studying the praying mantis, and I have three questions that I can't find answers to from my research. I thought maybe you could help me.

I have enclosed a self-addressed, stamped envelope for your convenience. Here are my questions:

    1. By what other names are praying mantises known?
    2. How many species are there?
    3. Can young praying mantises fly?

I appreciate any information you can provide about these questions. Thank you.

Sincerely,

John Jones

John Jones

EXAMPLE OF A "MODIFIED BLOCK LETTER" STYLE

Dr. David Adamson
Entomological Society
113 Geneva Road
Fair Ridge, OH 45289

March 22, 19XX

John Jones
1532 Hill Street
Bridgeton, TX 75588

Dear John,

I received your letter of March 16, and I am glad to help you. Here are my answers to your questions:

1. The praying mantis is also known by these names: rearhorse, mule killer, devil's horse, and soothsayer.
2. There are 20 species of praying mantis. The European mantis is well established in the eastern U.S., and the Chinese mantis has also established itself in the eastern states.
3. One female lays up to 1,000 eggs in the fall, which hatch in May or June. The young cannot fly; they grow slowly, acquiring wings and maturity in August. When mature, four well-developed wings allow slow, extended flight.

I hope this information helps you in your research work. By the way, thank you for enclosing a stamped envelope—I appreciate that. If I can be of further assistance, please let me know.

Sincerely,

David Adamson, M.D.

Dr. David Adamson

DEWEY DECIMAL CLASSIFICATION SYSTEM

1. The Dewey Decimal Classification System arranges all knowledge into ten "classes" numbered 0 through 9. Libraries use this system to assign a "call number" to every book in the building. A call number is simply an identification number that tells where a book is located in the library.

(000) 0—Generalities
(100) 1—Philosophy and related disciplines
(200) 2—Religion
(300) 3—The social sciences
(400) 4—Language
(500) 5—Pure sciences
(600) 6—Technology (applied sciences)
(700) 7—The arts
(800) 8—Literature and rhetoric
(900) 9—General geography, history,
        and so forth

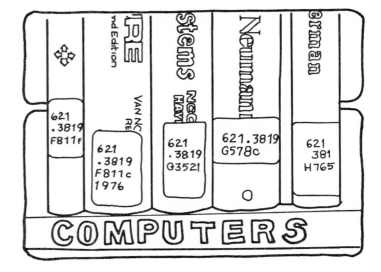

2. Each *class*, with the use of a three-digit number, is divided into ten subclasses (divisions) with the first division (600–609) set aside for the general works on the entire class. For example, 600–649:

600–609 is given over to *general works* on the applied sciences
610–619 to the medical sciences
620–629 to engineering and applied operations
630–639 to agriculture and agricultural industries
640–649 to domestic arts and sciences

3. Each division is separated into ten subclasses or *"sections"* with the first *"section"* (630) devoted to the general works on the entire *division*. For example:

630 is assigned to agriculture and agricultural industries in general
631 to farming activities
632 to plant diseases and pests and their control
633 to production of field crops
636 to livestock and domestic animals, etc.

4. Further subdividing is made by following the three-digit number with a decimal point and as many more digits as is necessary. For example, 631 farming is divided into

631.2 for farm structures
631.3 for farm tools, machinery, appliances
631.5 for crop production

5. In summary, every book in a library is assigned a call number based upon the Dewey Decimal Classification System. All library books are stored on shelves according to their numbers, making them easy to find.

6. To locate a book in the library follow these steps:

a. Use the card catalog to find the call number of a book in which you are interested. Books are cataloged by author, title, and subject.

b. Record the call number, usually recorded in the upper left-hand corner of the card. If your library uses a computerized catalog system, ask a librarian for assistance in locating the call number.

c. Refer to the first three numbers of the call number to determine in which section of the library your book can be found.

d. Once you have found this section of the library, use the rest of the call number to locate the book on the shelf.

THE CARD CATALOG

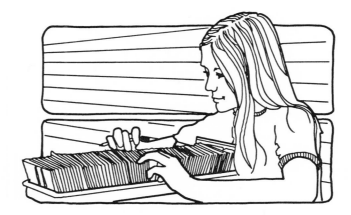

The card catalog is usually the first place you would go to look for a book in the library. The cards in the card catalog are arranged alphabetically by subject, author, and title. The card below is a "subject" card, filed under "inventors." The same book could be found if you looked under "Manchester, Harland Frank" (along with any other books Mr. Manchester has written) or *Trailblazers of Technology* (the title of the book).

Once you find the card that best fits your needs, the most important piece of information is the "call number" in the upper left-hand corner. This number tells you where to find the book in the library. In trying to decide which book to look up, you may refer to various pieces of information found on every catalog card. This information includes

1. Call number
2. Subject
3. Author
4. Author's birth date
5. Title
6. Brief description
7. Illustrator (if there is only one)

8. Location of publisher (city)
9. Publisher
10. Date of publication
11. Number of pages
12. Whether or not the book is illustrated
13. Size of the book

Here is a sample card:

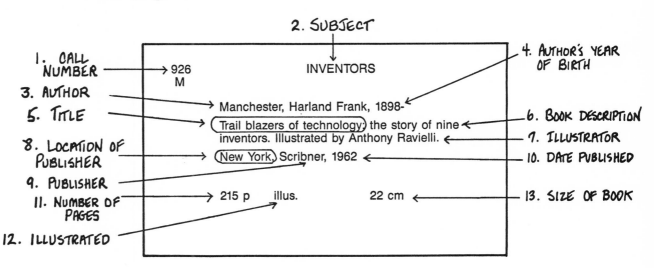

READERS' GUIDE TO PERIODICAL LITERATURE

The *Readers' Guide to Periodical Literature* is an extremely useful tool. You can find magazine articles about current topics from as recent as one or two months ago. You can also find articles that were written fifteen, twenty, or fifty years ago. Subject and author headings are arranged alphabetically in the *Guide*. Articles are arranged alphabetically under each heading.

When a promising reference is found, first determine how to locate the magazine that published the article. Does the library subscribe to the magazine? Is it a current issue? (Usually issues for the past twelve months will be available in the periodical reading section of the library.) Are old issues recorded on microfilm, or are they bound and placed in a special area of the library? When you find an article you want to read, record the following on a piece of paper. Then you or a librarian, if necessary, can locate the magazine from its file area.

The elements in each entry are:

1. Title of the article
2. Author's name
3. Name of the magazine
4. Volume number
5. Pages on which the article can be found
6. Date of publication

Suppose you are studying atomic power; specifically, you want to find out about the costs of building and operating atomic power plants. By looking through a *Readers' Guide*, you will find many articles published about atomic power. From the example provided you can see that "atomic bombs" is at the top of the list of atomic topics, followed by atomic energy, atomic energy industry, atomic facilities, atomic fuels, atomic power, atomic power industry, atomic power plants, and atomic research. There, under "Atomic power plants—Economic aspects," is a collection of five articles that could be useful to you. Look at the fourth one:

Whoops! A $2 billion blunder. C.P. Alexander. il *Time* 122:50-2 Ag 8 '83

1. Title: "Whoops! A $2 Billion Blunder"
2. Author: C.P. Alexander
3. il: this article is illustrated with photographs or drawings
4. Magazine: *Time*
5. Volume: 122
6. Page(s): 50-52
7. Date: August 8, 1983

The *Readers' Guide to Periodical Literature* makes use of abbreviations for months of the year, magazine names, and other pieces of important information. For example, "Bet Hom & Gard" is *Better Homes and Gardens* and "bi-m" means a magazine is published bimonthly. Be sure to refer to the first few pages of the *Readers' Guide* for a complete list of all the abbreviations used.

The following is a section from the *Readers' Guide to Periodical Literature.*

Atomic bombs
                  History
    See also
    Hiroshima (Japan)
            Physiological effects
    See Radiation—Physiological effects
            Testing
    See Atomic weapons—Testing
Atomic energy *See* Atomic power
Atomic energy industry *See* Atomic power industry
Atomic facilities *See* Nuclear facilities
Atomic fuels *See* Nuclear fuels
Atomic power
    See also
    Anti-nuclear movement
    Nuclear fuels
          Economic aspects
    See also
    Atomic power industry
          Laws and regulations
    See also
    Radioactive waste disposal—Laws and regulations
    Mixed rulings on nuclear power [Supreme Court decisions] R. Sandler. *Environment* 25:2-3 Jl/Ag '83
          Germany (West)
    See also
    Anti-nuclear movement—Germany (West)
Atomic power industry
    See also
    Computers—Atomic power industry use
    Reactor fuel reprocessing
    Washington Public Power Supply System
          Export-import trade
    Firing spotlights plutonium exports [R. Hesketh's claim that plutonium produced in Great Britain's civilian reactors has been used in U.S. weapons manufacture] D. Dickson. *Science* 221:245 Jl 15 '83
          Laws and regulations
    See Atomic power—Laws and regulations
          Public relations
    Atom and Eve [nuclear acceptance campaign geared to women] L. Nelson. il *Progressive* 47:32-4 Jl '83
          United States
    See Atomic power industry
Atomic power plants
          Economic aspects
    The bankruptcy of public power [Washington Public Power Supply System debacle] *Natl Rev* 35:982-3 Ag 19 '83
    Money meltdown [Washington Public Power Supply System default] S. Ridley. *New Repub* 189:11-13 Ag 29 '83
    When billions in bonds go bust [default of Washington Public Power Supply System] *U S News World Rep* 95:7 Ag 8 '83
    Whoops! A $2 billion blunder. C. P. Alexander. il *Time* 122:50-2 Ag 8 '83
    The Whoops bubble bursts. H. Anderson. il *Newsweek* 102:61-2 Ag 8 '83
          Laws and regulations
    See Atomic power—Laws and regulations
          Safety devices and measures
    Computers to supervise nuke plants. *Sci Dig* 91:27 Jl '83
Atomic research
    Pseudo-QCD [discussion of January 1983 article, A look at the future of particle physics] B. G. Levi. *Phys Today* 36:98+ Jl '83

Name _____ Date _____

CHOOSING A SUBJECT

The first step in any research project is choosing something to study. This requires some thought and decision making. This handout provides several guidelines that will help you select a subject.

1. Choose a subject that you are already interested in or that you would like to know more about.

2. Choose a subject that will meet the needs or requirements as outlined by the teacher:
   a. Listen for suggestions from the teacher.
   b. Be alert to ideas that come from class discussion.
   c. Talk to friends and parents about things you can study and learn.

3. A good rule by the Roman poet Horace: "Choose a subject, ye who write, suited to your strength." This means pick a subject you can understand, not one in which you will become bogged down, lost, or disinterested.

4. The encyclopedia should serve as a tool for choosing the right subject and narrowing it down so you can handle it:
   a. It gives the general areas of the subject.
   b. It identifies specific topics related to your subject.
   c. It is written simply enough to understand without hours of study.

5. Before you commit yourself to a subject, check to make sure there is some information available. There is nothing more frustrating than starting a project that cannot be finished because there are no books, magazines, filmstrips, newspapers, journals, experts, or even libraries that have enough information.

6. Once you have chosen a subject, write down a series of questions to which you want to find answers. Write as many as you can think of. These questions will help direct your research.

AUDIO-VISUAL AND WRITTEN INFORMATION GUIDES

DIRECTIONS: The following list shows some of the places where information can be found. When you begin your first project, go down column one and put a check mark in the box next to each place you *might* be able to find information. When you *do* find information, fill in the appropriate box on the chart with your pencil. Do this for your first five research projects.

	PROJECT NUMBER				
	1	2	3	4	5
Almanacs					
Atlases					
Bibliographies					
Biographies					
Charts and graphs					
Dictionaries					
Encyclopedias					
Films					
Filmstrips					
Historical stories					
Indexes to free material					
Letters					
Library card catalog					
Magazines					
Maps					
Microfilm					
Newspapers					
Pictures					
Readers' Guide to Periodical Literature					
Records					
Tapes					
Textbooks					
Vertical files					
Other:					

Name _____ Date _____

WHERE TO GO OR WRITE FOR INFORMATION

STONEHENGE

DIRECTIONS: Before you start your project, put a check mark in the box next to each place you could go or write to get information. When you *do* get information, fill in the appropriate box.

	PROJECT NUMBER				
	1	2	3	4	5
Chambers of Commerce					
Churches					
City officials					
Companies					
Embassies					
Experts					
Factories					
Federal agencies					
Historical societies					
Hobbyists					
Librarians					
Libraries					
Ministers					
Museums					
Newspaper office/employee					
Organizations (club, societies)					
Professionals					
Research laboratories					
State agencies					
Teachers					
Travel agencies					
Universities					
Zoos					
Friends					
Home (books, magazines, etc.)					
Other:					

Name _____ Date _____

PROJECT FACT SHEET

One of the most difficult parts of any project is getting started. Use the "Project Fact Sheet" to begin recording information that will be included in a presentation or report. A sample of a completed "Project Fact Sheet" is shown on the next page.

My topic is _____

and these are the facts I am going to teach the rest of the class:

1. _____

2. _____

3. _____

4. _____

5. _____

6. _____

7. _____

8. _____

9. _____

10. _____

11. _____

12. _____

13. _____

14. _____

15. _____

16. _____

17. _____

18. _____

19. _____

20. _____

PROJECT FACT SHEET: Example

This sample fact sheet about humpback whales shows how to write out information that is to be included in a presentation.

My topic is <u>Humpback Whales,</u> and these are the facts I am going to teach the rest of the class:

1. Humpback whales spend six months in the South Pacific.
2. Humpback whales sing a strange song that seems to be some sort of communication.
3. Humpback whales sing only when they are in the South Pacific.
4. Humpback whales do not eat when they are in the South Pacific.
5. Humpback whales travel to an arctic Alaskan bay to feed.
6. A humpback whale has a brain that is five times larger than a human brain.
7. The invention of the explosive harpoon gun and the steam engine made full-scale hunting of the humpback whale possible.
8. Humpback whales show great devotion to one another; this is best displayed by the relationship between a mother and her young.
9. A young whale is called a "calf."
10. The humpback whale eats krill, which makes it a carnivorous mammal.
11. (This list is extended to whatever the project outline requires.)

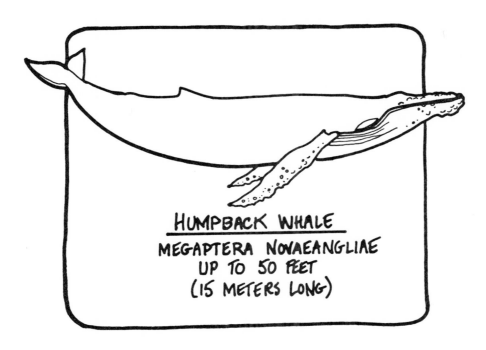

HUMPBACK WHALE
MEGAPTERA NOVAEANGLIAE
UP TO 50 FEET
(15 METERS LONG)

POSTER DISPLAY SHEET

Use the guidelines on this handout if you are required to make a poster for a research project.

1. Present or "teach" at least twenty facts about your topic on the poster. These facts should be recorded on notecards.

2. The poster should be made to go with the written report so that they can be used together when you make a presentation.

3. Include at least one of your own drawings on it.

4. The poster can also have other pictures, magazine articles, newspaper headlines, quotes from books, charts, graphs, illustrations, explanations, diagrams, captions, and so forth.

5. Organize all of the material on the poster so that it is easy to understand. This is very important when making a top-quality poster. Give your poster visual impact by using colorful designs, bold headings, and a catchy title.

6. Writing must be neat! Use parallel guidelines and pencil words in lightly before going over them with marker.

7. Check spelling, grammar, capitalization, punctuation, and sentences to be sure they are correct.

8. Every bit of information you use must be accurate. *Do not make anything up!*

9. Your poster should be about a very specific topic. Don't throw everything you can find onto it. Be selective and use only material that contributes favorably to the project.

10. OPTIONAL: Write five questions that can be answered by studying your poster. These questions should be attached to the poster.

Name _____ Date _____

THINGS TO CHECK BEFORE GIVING YOUR PRESENTATION

DIRECTIONS: After practicing your presentation at home one time, write "yes" or "no" in the boxes below to help determine which areas need more work. The purpose of this checklist is to help put *quality* into your presentation. Use it wisely and be honest. If something needs more time and effort, be willing to admit it and work to improve what you have done.

	PROJECT NUMBER				
	1	2	3	4	5
Have I done enough research?					
Is everything spelled correctly?					
Did I use neat handwriting?					
Is everything in my visual display labeled?					
Do all my pictures have captions?					
Is my visual display neat and attractive?					
Did I use colors in a pleasing way?					
Did I do my best artwork?					
Does my oral report need more practice?					
Do I know all the words in my report?					
Is it easy to understand what I have written?					
Is my report informative?					
Is my visual display informative?					
Do I understand the information I will present?					
Did I choose interesting and different presentation methods?					
Have I decided how I will display my visual materials during my presentation?					
Am I ready to answer questions about my subject?					
Did I follow the project directions or outline?					
Does my presentation stick to my subject?					
Is this my best work?					

Name _____ Date _____

VISUAL AIDS FOR THE ORAL PRESENTATION

DIRECTIONS: Making your report interesting is very important. Besides hearing what you have to say, the audience likes to see examples of what you've done. There are many ways to use visual aids during a presentation. This list provides some suggestions. First, check the items that you think you *could* use. Later, fill in the ones you actually *did* use.

	PROJECT NUMBER				
	1	2	3	4	5
Chalkboard					
Charts					
Clippings					
Diagrams					
Dioramas					
Film (slides)					
Filmstrips					
Guest speakers					
Magazines					
Maps					
Models					
Murals					
Opaque projector					
Overhead projector					
Pictures					
Posters					
Records					
Tape recorder					
Other: _____					
_____					

When speaking to a group you must always be aware of these things:

1. Voice projection
2. Eye contact
3. Inflection

4. Proper grammar
5. Hand control
6. Posture

THINGS TO REMEMBER
WHEN PRESENTING YOUR PROJECT

Try to remember these rules when you are speaking before the group. Underline the ones you need to improve. On the lines at the bottom of this sheet, write any other rules and notes you feel you need as reminders.

1. Speak in complete sentences.
2. Use any new vocabulary words you may have learned, but be sure you can pronounce them and that you know what they mean.
3. Speak with a clear voice so that everyone can hear.
4. Look at your audience and speak to its members.
5. Stand aside when you are pointing out pictures, maps, charts, drawings, or diagrams.
6. Do not read long passages from your notes.
7. Know your material so that you sound like an informed person.
8. Be as calm as possible. Try to show that you have confidence in your work.
9. Do not chew gum when presenting.
10. Be ready to tell where you got your information.
11. Explain what your visual display shows, but don't read everything that is on it to your audience. Let the audience read it later.
12. Ask for questions from the class.
13. Be willing to admit that you don't know an answer if you really don't know.
14. Never make up an answer. You are expected to give only accurate information.
15. When your project is due to be presented, have it ready in final form—and on time! Do not come to class with empty hands and a list of excuses.

16. _____

_____

17. _____

_____

18. _____

_____

NOTES: _____

_____

_____

© 1987 by The Center for Applied Research in Education, Inc.